# EDUCATION FOR THE SOUL
## Behind the Prison Walls

# DEDICATION

*"And we know that God causes everything to work together*
*for the good of those who love God*
*and are called according to His purpose for them.*

**Romans 8:28**

I dedicate this book *Education for the Soul behind the Prison Walls* to Mr. Edwin C. Wilson, former Educational Officer with Her Majesty's Prison and former Commissioner of Prisons. In 1984, Mr. Wilson in his wisdom contacted me and asked if I would assist in teaching at the prison facilities with my GED and computer programmes.

With his wisdom, knowledge, insight, and skills as a former teacher, he had a vision for those behind the prison walls to get their high school diplomas in addition to computer education and typing skills. I am indebted to him for hiring me in 1984 because the success of the programme was a result of his dedication to education. In his own life, Mr. Wison had mountains to climb, and he successfully climbed over and through all of them.

At the time, my learning centre had recently opened its doors to the community, and I did not hesitate to accept the offer to teach in the prison facilities because I knew firsthand that there were individuals behind the prison walls who needed education. At that time, I was tutoring my cousin who had been incarcerated; when he was released, he needed to ugrade his skills. As a matter of fact, he was the very first student to enroll at C.A.R.E. Computer Services.

I am very thankful for the opportunity that Mr. Wilson afforded me, and I appreciated his assistance because he allowed me to teach and be flexible wth the curriculum I had for the inmates. It was an honour to do my thing and set educational goals for all the inmates enrolled.

My first class was held at the Senior Training School for Boys behind St. George's Opera House, and I traveled there weekly with a van packed full of computers because, at that time, computers were new to the prisons and Bermuda's education department. I recall one day when a fight broke out in the classroom and rather than try to stop the fight, the students and I were busy securing the computers to prevent them from falling off the tables onto the floor and crashing to pieces. The class was held in the visiting room, so the prison officers were nearby and were very quick to secure the boys who were fighting, and after some disruption, the class resumed until finishing time.

Soon after I began teaching at the Training School, word got out to other prison facilities about our success and the level of interest in the classes. Because both of the courses were new, they requested that Mr. Wilson provide the same instruction at the Prison Farm and the Women's Prison in Prospect, Devonshire.

Mr. Wilson approached me, and we discussed the possibilities and how I would assist in accommodating the other facilities. I accepted the challenge and found the days and times to teach. Teaching at the three facilities went on for about a year, and inmates (students) started to excel in their studies. Success was on the horizon with several students completing the GED requirements and receiving their high school diplomas; this success was not only exciting but emotional as well.

After a year of success, Mr. Wilson was ever so thankful. If anyone in the administration had any complaints or concerns about the school supplies and tools for learning that the students requested, Mr. Wilson was right there to sort things out, and he made sure the students got what they needed. I was ever so grateful for his assistance and understanding. He even gave me a key to the supply cabinet that contained all the tools, from calculators to pencils, pens, and GED textbooks. With that access, classes went on very smoothly and, of course, inmates had to be responsible for the supplies they received because I kept an account of those who received supplies for Mr. Wilson's review.

I don't think Mr. Wilson anticipated that those behind the prison walls would be so receptive to educational development. But with the growing need, he became a very busy Educational Officer. Mr. Wilson was the first Educational Officer to be hired by government, the Ministry of Health and Social Services, and his work and appreciation have not gone unnoticed by me and others who recall his works during a new season of education behind the prison walls.

With the success of the programmes, there was one more facility that did not want to be left out of receiving educational courses, and that was Casemates Prison. How could Mr. Wilson not accommodate Casemates Prison? At that time, there was tension there, and something positive had to be done to assist the inmates. While classes such as English, math, carpentry, sewing, Bible studies, and more were being taught, no one was teaching the GED and computer training.

Those courses were new to all and, with much traveling from St. George's to Dockyard, education for the souls behind the prison walls flourished, and I am thankful and appreciative that it continues today. Over 150 inmates received their GED (high school diploma), and over 500 received computer instruction under my tutelage.

Mr. Wilson, in his wisdom, knew that studies have shown that inmate participation in educational, vocational training, prison work skills development and programmes reduces recidivism. And that proved to be true in our case. Many of those who took the courses and were successful did not return to prison or a life of crime but returned to society as positive men and women.

A special thanks to the Prison Administration, Commissioners of Prison, Chief Officers, Principal Officers, Prison Officers, staff, Prison Fellowship Bermuda, Treatment of Offenders Board, and the volunteers and special speakers from the community who shared in the development of inmates. Thanks to Bermuda College for assisting this effort by administering inmate testing on the campus in Devonshire and for allowing the inmates to use their graduation gowns and caps in our graduation ceremonies. Bermuda College also offered courses on higher education subjects such as College Preparation to those who passed their GED examinations.

I will always cherish the opportunity that was given to me by Mr. Wilson because, with his vision, the educational programmes behind the prison walls helped to make inmates stronger and smarter. Because of their mistakes in life, they are wiser in making better decisions today. Many ex-prisoners say that education improved their cognitive functions and helped them to reduce the antisocial attitudes and behaviours associated with their criminal behaviour. Education also helped them disengage from a prison mentality and create positive goals and a meaningful life in the right direction.

Mr. Edwin Cleeve Wilson, BA, MA, MBE, you have done so much for our island home; dedicating this book to you has been an honour and a blessing. God doesn't give us what we can handle. God helps us handle what we are given, and I know that you have a law degree and could have gone on to be one of Bermuda's outstanding lawyers, but you chose to work with those individuals behind the prison walls. *"THE LORD IS CLOSE TO THE BROKENHEARTED; HE RESCUES THOSE WHOSE SPIRITS ARE CRUSHED"* (Psalm 34:18).

Many thanks for giving me the opportunity to touch the souls of those behind the prison walls with love, care, and appreciation.

Hon. D. Neletha Butterfield, M.B.E., J.P.

# FOREWORD

*"For people who have committed crimes that have landed them in jail*
*There needs to be a path back from prison*
*The federal system of parole needs to be reinstated*
*We need real education and real skills training for the incarcerated."*

**—Senator Berne Sanders**

In 1984, I was asked by the newly appointed Educational Officer, Mr. Edwin C. Wilson, if I would like to bring the GED Preparation Course and Computer Skills Programme to the correctional facilities. I readily accepted and after two years in the programme approximately 24 inmates received their high school diplomas and over 50 received computer skills including typing skills. Rather than have this Foreword written by someone else, I thought it fitting and different to use this letter from a former inmate to describe the significance of education behind the prison walls; the letter was written and received on October 3, 1986.

*Casemates Prison*
*Ireland Island*
*10/3/86*

*8 West Park Lane*
*Pembroke West*
*Bermuda*

*Dear Mrs. Williams,*

*I write with hope that this letter finds you and your family at your best. Last week seem to have been like two weeks in one and will describe your absence as if myself and others had lost our best friend, or more like a broken romance. "Smile"*

*Your presence at Casemates has made Tuesdays and Fridays two special outstanding days behind these walls, and I like the others have become addicted to your warm and sound attitude. I've also found out that we are not the only ones that depend on your appearance because when talking with the Commissioner last week, he spoke very good of you and Deputy Commissioner Fraser, upheld you with high esteem and how your ins and outs at P.H.O. (Prison Headquarters Office) are solid, commenting how your interest for your students at the prison being priceless and genuine.*

*I know and accept that you have a very wide scope to cover and do understand that you are only human, therefore, I have added you in my prayers, that the good "Lord" bless, guide and protect you and that all good things come on to you.*

*May love peace and understanding be with you.*

*Always,*
*Your student*
*Cleveland M. Simmons*

Cleveland received his high school diploma (GED) in 1986 and also received certificates in computer skills, computer programming, and typing skills. He was an outstanding student willing to learn, and he encouraged others who were incarcerated to join the classes, especially the younger men who needed to upgrade their educational skills in reading and mathematics. A special thanks: I have been blessed in many ways with his friendship and love as he continues to share his educational experience behind the prison walls with others today.

# INTRODUCTION

*"Ambition is the desire to go forward and improve one's condition.*
*It is a burning flame that lights up the life of the individual*
*And makes him see himself in another state.*
*To be ambitious is to be great in mind and soul.*
*To want that which is worthwhile and strive for it.*
*To go on without looking back, reaching to that which gives satisfaction."*

**—Marcus Garvey**

I taught in the prisons for approximately 20 years. I remember when I was working with students years back, a young man who was exceptionally good with mathematics asked, "Why are we doing algebra?" I had to explain to him that we use mathematics every day to live and survive financially and economically. I shared about a few careers that require knowing as much mathematics as possible. For example, I told him, an airplane pilot or the captain of a ship needs to know coordinates in order to give his location. He looked at me and said that no one had ever told him that before. Another student had to write an essay on the topic "Why I Want My GED." He wrote in his essay that his teacher always reminded him that he would grow up to be nothing but a street sweeper. I was floored, and I gasped when I read his essay; I felt his pain and sensed why he wanted to change his life through education. I quickly purchased a book on the life of Rev. Dr. Martin Luther King, Jr. and wrote these words of encouragement inside the cover of the book: *"If a man is called to be a street sweeper, he should sweep streets even as a Michelangelo painted, or Beethoven composed music or Shakespeare wrote poetry. He should sweep streets so well that all the hosts of heaven and earth will pause to say, 'Here lived a great street sweeper who did his job well.'* The student asked, "Ms. Butterfield did he really say that?" I replied, "Read the book." He read the book and found the speech in which Dr. King made that statement. This inspired him, and he enrolled in the GED class and received his high school diploma.

That was a real turning point for my career teaching behind the prison walls. So, I tried always to remember these students and reflect that in how I taught. When you're proud of a student's accomplishments in anything, it's very important to tell them how others overcame, especially people that they can relate to. So many in the community prayed for me as this was not an easy journey. Seeing so many individuals incarcerated and such a high percentage of them returning to prison was very heartbreaking, but sharing my experience was very helpful.

A senior citizen friend wrote these words to me in a note in 1986: *"Dear Neletha, many thanks for taking me with you to the Co-Ed Correctional Facility graduation ceremony; that was the best graduation I have ever seen. God bless you; keep up the good work. Remember to keep pressing on, Love Mom Warner."*

*Education for the Soul Behind the Prison Walls* gives an account of the accomplishments and the successes of the inmates who attended classes and graduated with their high school diplomas and computer skills certificates. To all those I taught behind the prison walls, I can say that I am very thankful because you expressed your appreciation and to this day, former students stop me along the streets to say thanks or visit me at my learning centre because I am now teaching or have taught their sons and daughters and, now, their grandchildren. I chuckle when I make note of this because the children say, "You look too young to have taught my father, mother, grandfather or grandmother." However, time is of the essence, and I am very grateful for the opportunity to have changed their lives around, and they are living a positive life now because of education. I say to them, "For the good times, with a smile." I recall good times such as when Good Friday was approaching, and the inmates freely made over a hundred kites to give to the children in the community. There was no charge; they just made the kites with care and a touch of love. Today, there is a price for what the inmates make, and I can understand why. But there is a story to be told of the way inmates freely gave of their time and service back in the day.

There were good times and bad times and many challenges teaching in the prison. One of the inmates wrote a thank you note expressing how much the GED programme meant to him: "*Thank you for the quality time you put in me and more importantly for all the good work that you continue to contribute to the people of Bermuda. It will not go unnoticed.*" This note was from an inmate I taught to read and learn computers. I received this note via airmail on September 20, 2006 approximately four years after I stopped teaching at the correctional facilities. This young man now resides in England. This note of thanks brought tears to my eyes because before his release, this inmate seemed destined to be in a mental institution. Thank God for His mercy and His grace that this young man overcame his illness and was restored.

I trust that the readers of this book will be inspired and recognize that there is hope in spite of one's situation. We all know of someone who has been incarcerated a friend, family member, son, daughter, colleague, or a special loved one, but whom through rehabilitation and restoration, was restored. Through forgiveness, we are forgiven. Let us continue to listen to others' problems and spend time with people who are struggling for redemption and restoration, especially those who will, at some time in life, be released from prison.

Hon. D. Neletha Butterfield, M.B.E., J.P.

# CONTENTS

# PRISON FELLOWSHIP BERMUDA

1984
"Beyond Crime and Punishment"

*"Our character is determined not by our circumstances
but by our reaction to those circumstances"*

**—Chuck Colson, Founder Prison Fellowship International**

As I introduced the GED Preparation Programme in Her Majesty's Prison for the first time, the thirst for education in the prisons was exploding with excitement for the inmates and prison administration, and the news media was enthusiastic about getting this information out to the public.

In 1984, educational programmes had already started with much success at the Senior Training School for Boys in St. George's (located behind St. George's Opera Theatre), the Prison Farm at Ferry Reach, and the Women's Prison in Prospect, Devonshire. With much success and with enrollment matching the highest level of classroom accommodation, the Educational Officer, Mr. Edwin Wilson, asked if I could teach courses at Casemates Prison.

I accepted willingly because I believed that, in some instances, a prisoner's journey is easily forgotten or marginalized. If we are to assist in rescuing the vulnerable, reprove offenders, and restore peace and justice in the prison community, I had a duty to also help those at the Casemates Prison.

Initially, teaching at Casemates Prison was a very challenging experience. The classroom was very dingy, desperately needing something to make it conducive to learning. Windows were cracked, panes were missing, and the bathroom wasn't one that you would invite anyone to use. However, we had a chapel with a piano and hymn books; this was a solace place for some of the inmates. Often, someone was there who played the piano to tunes that blessed us immensely along with the melodious male voices singing hymns. I felt their passion and forgiveness and remorse for the crimes they had committed; it made me very comfortable to be in their presence.

A *Royal Gazette* reporter came to interview me and the students in the class. Through that article, I requested that the community get involved and volunteer their services in the prison. As a result, someone called to volunteer. That person was none other than Mr. Jack Harris who was working at Willowbank Hotel at the time. Thus, Jack and I began a friendship behind the prison walls. He volunteered his time to teach English and business courses. It has been said that prison ministry is not a job or Sunday routine. It is a privilege to be chosen and used by Jesus to go in the prison and teach.

Jack and I had lunches and meetings to discuss forming Prison Fellowship Bermuda. Prison Fellowship International (now called Prison Fellowship Ministries) is based in United States of America founded by Chuck Colson in 1976 after he was sent to prison for his involvement in the Watergate affair. While incarcerated, Mr. Colson saw the toll that crime takes on victims and communities; he saw that prison alone turns few lives around but, when a prisoner's life transforms, it changes the story for everyone. Prison Fellowship Ministries (PFM) has become the world's largest outreach to prisoners, ex-prisoners, crime victims, and their families.

In 1984, the Bermuda Branch of Prison Fellowship was introduced by me, the Hon. Neletha Butterfield. I was teaching at Casemates Prison when Prison Fellowship Bermuda (PFB) was formed, and Jack Harris taught and visited the inmates. Having heard of Chuck Colson's work in collaboration with churches of all confessions and denominations, we obtained the Prison Fellowship Charter in 1989. PFB believes that all people have value, deserve mercy, and are loved equally by God, even the most outcast. PFB helps to restore hope and share God's redeeming grace with prisoners and their families in Bermuda.

I am ever so thankful to the volunteers who are still keeping Prison Fellowship Bermuda going as a charity and ever so pleased to know that the vision has been passed on to others. May they continue to minister to those behind the prison walls at the Prison Farm, Co-Ed Correctional Facility, and Westgate Correctional Facility. Rev. Martin Luther King said," *Life's most urgent and persistent question is what are you doing for others?"*

There are those in the community who feel that nothing should be done for those who are incarcerated, but there are so many stories and testimonies of volunteers as well as prisoners who turn their lives around and witness to others while they are in prison and once released. Here is the story of a released prisoner; I believe former inmates are the best individuals to help to change other prisoners' lives.

> John's brother-in-law Michael was arrested for importation of drugs and was imprisoned for five years. During that time, Michael found a commitment to serve God, and he dedicated himself to sharing Christ's love with fellow inmates. When Michael was released, John took him in. Michael shared many stories with John about the forgotten prisoners, and John wanted to find ways that he could help.
>
> A door opened for John and Michael with Prison Fellowship Bermuda, and they shared the gospel with the inmates. Supported by his family, Michael daily trusts God to guide him in ministering to prisoners, even after they are released. Today, Michael also preaches in and out of prison, runs a business, teaches Bible study, and

ministers in song. He thanks God for allowing him to give something back to the community.

I had the honour and privilege of teaching Michael. He received his GED and is a licensed evangelist.

*"Continue to remember those in prison as if you were together with them in prison and those who are mistreated as if you yourselves were suffering."*

**—Hebrews 13:3**

# INMATES LEARN ALL ABOUT BEING 'USER FRIENDLY'

From the roadside it seems innocent enough—a beige house with white blinds—but once the door is opened, it's a totally new world.

Maybe it was fate, but to Ms. Neletha Williams and her students in the CARE (Children and Adults Reaching for Education) academic programme, it was destiny.

For the past four years, a 34-year-old North Shore, Pembroke, woman has given the term 'user friendly' a whole new meaning. She has transformed her own home into a computer centre while still using it as her residence. Along the walls of the lower lab, there are nine terminals and another six in the upper lab.

The former accountant, now working as a computer assistant instruction consultant, has taken her talents to teach youngsters and adults all about computers. And her own enthusiasm has even gone beyond the confines of her house/school.

Her day begins at 9 a.m. with a trip in her fully stocked van to go behind the walls of Casemates and teach inmates courses that include mathematics and practical reading skills in the high school diploma programme. In addition, she also spends time with inmates at the Prison Farm. In all, about 50 inmates take advantage of her classes.

By noon, she is winding down and making her way back to the city in preparation for another after-school session with youngsters.

Ms. Williams says: "I'm not looking for glory, for God has created me for his glory, and if I can help someone along the way, then my living is not in vain."

She first started helping her daughter, who was having some problems with her schoolwork and realized that there are others who shared the same problem.

Rather than being selfish, Ms. Williams used her expertise to teach an after-school class and admits that she even learns a bit from her students.

One of her challenges is helping the inmates learn more about the functions of the computer.

Her efforts have not gone unrewarded. Her students enjoy a high success rate for completing their high school diploma and other computer courses. That's all the thanks Ms. Williams is looking for.

In last year's class, 20 out of 24 inmates successfully passed their high school examination, and there is an annual graduation ceremony for the students.

There has been positive feedback from the Commissioner and Assistant Commissioner of Prisons and from members of the public concerning her computer classes.

She says: "I would like to see the prisoners get back into society having had an opportunity to learn something during their incarceration and prepared to show their worth when released."

Her main hope is that there would be a sponsor who would provide the all-important software for the classes held at the prison.

She bought her terminals one at a time and without government funding. All the money has come out of her own pocket.

Her door is always open to those wanting to volunteer their services, and parents are encouraged to sit in on the tutoring sessions in order to appreciate the system.

"Children and Adults Reaching for Education is what CARE is all about," says Mrs. Williams.

# U. B. P.

Dr. Hon. C. E. James, J. P., M. P., Chairman

Hon. Ann F. Cartwright DeCouto, J. P., M. P.

9th May, 1986

Mrs. Neletha Williams,

Director, Consultant, C.A.I. Instructor, C.A.R.E. Computer Services,

8 West Park Lane,

Pembroke West

Dear Mrs. Williams,

Thank you very much for your letter of the 28th April, 1986, enclosing the bulletin outlining the first Casemates Graduation Programme.

I am extremely pleased at the success that you have achieved with these inmates and know that it can be attributed a great deal to your dedication and hard work, as well as to your enthusiasm that has inspired them. ,

Again, heartiest congratulations.

Yours sincerely,

Ann F. Cartwright DeCouto, J.P., M

SPEAKER'S CHAMBERS
BERMUDA

Ref.:  GA-90-1

14th May, 1986

Mrs. Aletha Williams
8 West Park Lane
Pembroke 5

Dear Mrs. Williams,

At the meeting of the House of Assembly on Friday, 9th May, Mr. R. A. Burrows, J.P., M.P. asked that the congratulations of the House be sent to you on the excellent educational work that you have done at Casemates Prison. The prisoners have greatly benefited from your dedication and skill.

In carrying out the wishes of the House may I add my own personal congratulations on your valuable contribution towards the rehabilitation of the prisoners.

Yours sincerely,

F. J. BARRITT, C.B.E., J.P., M.P.
SPEAKER

# GRADUATION CLASS OF 1986 – PRISON FARM AND CO-ED

8ᵗʰ December, 1986

*"In all thy ways acknowledge Him and He shall direct your paths"*

**—Proverbs 3: 6**

The second Annual Graduation was held at the Co-Ed Correctional Facility for both the Prison Farm and Co-Ed students of the GED class. The guest speaker was Dr. Rev. Vernon Lambe Sr. The ceremony was attended by family, friends, prison administration, and Ms. Sherri Bridgewater, Assistant Director of Student Services at the Bermuda College. Students and graduates participated in the programme as the master of ceremonies, welcome, musical selections, and a vote of thanks. A total of 10 inmates received their GED (high school diploma).

**Graduates Pledge**

As one of the graduates of this 1986 GED class, I would like to express my utmost gratitude to all those involved in making this moment possible for myself and for all other graduates who are present. To pass this exam was a great satisfaction for me, and I am sure it was the same for all of the others who graduated with me.

So we the graduates would like you all to know that we are grateful for your support and feel proud to accept these certificates, with the hope that future inmates may know the satisfaction of achieving a meaningful goal such as this and will take the opportunity to stabilize their lives through education.

We, the graduates, pledge to enhance, encourage and support good educational programmes with the philosophy that education is the key to eliminating ignorance.

**—By Leigh Hall – Graduate 1986**

**Graduates of 1986 Class – Prison Farm**

Leroy Brangman    Leigh Hall
Elroy Dill    Jerome Laws
Brian Gibbons

## Graduates Pledge – Co-Ed Correctional Facility

We all cannot be famous
or be listed in the Who's Who
But every person great or small
has important things to do
For seldom do we realize
The importance of small deeds
or to what success or greatness
unnoticed kindness leads
For it is not the big celebrity
in a world of fame and praise
but it is doing unpretentiously
in undistinguished ways
the works that God assigned to us
unimportant as it seems
that makes our task understanding
and brings reality to dreams
this old world would very soon
follow the guiding star
If everybody brightened up
The corner where they are – **This is our pledge to you**

## Graduates of 1986 Class – Co-Ed Facility

Leslie Grant          David Trott

Warren Mallory        Dean Young

Brian Trott

## Instructor's Message

Sincere congratulations to you, the graduates of the Class of '87. This evening ceremony symbolizes the joy and success which you are experiencing. I ask, that you continue your education development, being careful to learn from others, making sure that you teach yourself. Be industrious and cultivate your own self-esteem. May your continuing efforts bring greater success to each one of you and profit the community in which you choose to live and work.

I am thankful to God for inspiring me to be of assistance to you, and my prayer is that your accomplishments have provided that solid foundation that you need in order to meet life's challenges with confidence and strength.

Remember, "In all thy ways acknowledge Him and He shall direct your paths" (Proverbs 3:6).

**—Neletha Williams – GED Instructor /Computer Consultant**

# GRADUATION CLASS OF 1986 – CASEMATES PRISON

11th December, 1986

*"Not by might, nor my power but by my spirit."*

—Zechariah 4:6

## Graduates Pledge

In the past, we had hoped that future inmates would know the satisfaction of achieving a meaningful goal and because of the past, we now know that we can achieve that goal. So, we, the graduates, pledge to enhance and support good educational programmes with the philosophy that education is the key to eliminating ignorance that we can overcome.

**By Raymond Grant – Graduate 1986**

## Graduates of 1986 Class

Archibald Douglas    Cleveland Simmons
Kevin Gibbons        Robert Trott
Raymond Grant        Paul Viera

Give it all you've got
Resist evil, learn to say no
Affirm that you can do it
Dare to try, dare to love, dare to be different
Unlock some human values – faith, hope and love
Attitude – accept instruction with an open mind
Time how to use it
Educate yourself, keep getting smarter
Share the credit and share the glory

**Love, Neletha Williams**

Hon D. Neletha Butterfield, M.B.E., J.P.

## Class of '86 Graduation Programme
### 6th December, 1986

MASTER OF CEREMONIES :    Roger Lightbourne

OPENING HYMN :           "SHOWERS OF BLESSINGS"
OPENING PRAYER :         Waunda Henry

WELCOME :                Sandra Davis (Co-Ed)
                         William Richardson (P.Farm)
SELECTION :              Deana Moniz

INTRODUCTION OF SPEAKER :   Leslie Grant
SELECTION:                  Beverly Swann

SPEAKER:                 DR. REV. VERNON LAMBE

### PRESENTATION OF CERTIFICATES & AWARDS

SELECTION :              Sandra Davis
REMARKS :                Mr. Edwin Wilson
                         Educational Officer
                         H.M. Prisons
REMARKS :                Miss Sherri Bridgewater
                         Bda. College (Asst. Director
                         Student Services)
VOTE OF THANKS :         Yusef DeSilva (Co-Ed)
                         Leroy Brangman (Pr. Farm)
PRESENTATION :           Dean Young (Co-Ed)
                         Gene Bean (Prison Farm)

INSTRUCTOR'S MESSAGE
--------------------

    Sincere congratulations to you, the graduates
of the Class of ' 86. This evening's ceremony
symbolizes the joy and success which you have
experienced. I ask, that you continue your
education development, being careful to learn
from others, and making sure that you teach yourself. Be industrious and cultivate your own self-
esteem. May your continuing efforts bring greater
success to each of you and profit the community
in which you choose to live and work.
    I am thankful to God for inspiring me to be of
assistance to you and my prayer is that your
accomplishments have provided that solid
foundation that you will need in order to meet life's
chanllenges with confidence and strength. Remember,
"In all ways acknowledge him and he shall direct
your paths." Proverbs 3:6


Neletha Williams
G.E.D.* Instructor/Computer Consultant


GRADUATES PLEDGE * CO-ED FACILITY
<<<<<<<<<<<<<<<<<<<>>>>>>>>>>>>>>>>>

         We all cannot be famous
         or be listed in who's who
       But every person great or small
          has important things to do
          For seldom do we realize
        the importance of small deeds
       or to what success of greatness
          unnoticed kindness leads
       For it's not the big celebrity
        in a world of fame and praise
         but its doing unpretentiously
           In undistinguished ways
       the works that God assigned to us
           Unimportant as it seems
        that makes our task understanding
         and brings reality to dreams
        this old world would very soon
           follow the guiding star
         If everybody brightened up
          The corner where they are

THIS OUR PLEDGE TO YOU,

12

*Premier*

The Cabinet Office
Hamilton 5-24, Bermuda
19th January, 1987.

Ms. Neletha Williams,
Director/Computer Consultant/G.E.D. Instructor,
C.A.R.E. Computer Services,
8 West Park Lane,
Pembroke 07.

Dear Ms. Williams:

This is to acknowledge your letter of 18th December, 1986 and to thank you for sending me copies of the programmes of the recent graduation of students (inmates) at Casemates Prison.

I am pleased to hear that 16 graduates have received High School Diplomas and would be grateful if you would convey my congratulations to them. I am sure this achievement will go a long way in helping them succeed in their future endeavours.

Your encouragement and support has, I am sure, been of tremendous benefit to the inmates, and I wish you much success as you continue with this worthwhile project.

Yours sincerely,

John W. Swan

*Premier*

*The Cabinet Office*
*Hamilton 5-24, Bermuda*

27th August, 1987.

Ms. Neletha Williams,
Director/Accountant/Computer Consultant,
C.A.R.E. Computer Services,
8 West Park Lane,
Pembroke West HM 07.

Dear Ms. Williams:

Thank you for your letter of 19th August, 1987 and for sending me the brochure entitled "Woman to Woman: Single Parenting from a Global Perspective".

I am pleased to hear that your attendance at the conference was a rewarding and stimulating experience. I am sure your presentation topic "Exciting, Enhancing, Enriching and Encouraging Education with Computers" was well received by the participants.

I would like to take this opportunity to congratulate you for your efforts on behalf of our country at the conference.

Best wishes for continued success in your endeavours.

Yours sincerely,

John W. Swan

Casemates Prison
Ireland Island
4/4/87

Attention: Mr. Chairman
Chairman of Bethel A.M.E. Church Men's Day
Shelly Bay, Hamilton Parish.

Dear Mr. Chairman,

We the inmates of the above mentioned address take this time out for the inmates in the education class to express our sincere thanks for the support the church has given us over the last year.

We personally cannot be with you on this day. However, we would like for you to know we are with you in spirit and truth in looking forward as men to be in the number, when the saints go marching on.

With our profound support we render this small contribution towards your work for Almighty God.

Enclosed you will find a dollar for each inmate that is being taught by one of your church-sisters who teaches not only education, but also that Jesus died to forgive all from sin that repent.

May you have a successful Men's Day in the name and honour of Jesus Christ.

Respectfully yours,

Inmates of Casemates

# COMPUTER MAKES A DIFFERENCE TO LIFE AT CASEMATES

20th April, 1987

Whether it is rain, wind blow, or shine, 9:30 a.m. Tuesdays and Fridays cannot come soon enough for the computer class students at Casemates Prison. For these inmates, life behind bars is more tolerable when it's time for school. Anticipation is keen, and many talk about what they are going to do when they receive their diploma before returning to the "**real world**." Convicted rapists, drug smugglers, and murderers turn their talents to practical reading skills and word processing rather than sitting in a cell waiting for the world to go by. Some of the inmates—serving sentences of up to 18 years—spend their time studying for a college degree.

Spearheading the class is 34-year-old Ms. Neletha Williams who divides her time between teaching inmates at Casemates, the Prison Farm, the Senior Training School for Boys, and the Women's Prison. Her teaching has spread beyond the confines of her North Shore, Pembroke, school/home, and her efforts have not been in vain.

One inmate who is studying for his GED (high school diploma) said many of the guys are interested in the computer class, but having access to a computer is very limited. He said: "There's no software here, only what Ms. Williams brings. I wish there was some public funding to increase what we have." One prison officer said about 30 percent of the inmates are functionally illiterate, but they are encouraged to take advantage of the classes offered, space permitting.

The remedial reading programme at Casemates is designed to create a balance for the streetwise person who never took an education seriously. One student said: "My main thing is leaving here and showing them that I will not fall. Right now, my reading isn't up to snuff, but it will be when I leave. We really need more teachers in this area." The class of some 20 men shares two computers and works on such subjects as English, math, and, sometimes science. All of the men hope to donate something to expand the class once they are released so others will be able to take advantage of the programme. One student said: "These programmes make you of some value to society, and the progress is beginning to show." The remedial class runs along with the GED programme and the students agree that their vocabulary has increased and they are not as bad off as they originally thought.

Some of the inmates write their own programmes, sometimes making music with the aid of a computer. One inmate who has had some experience with computers said: "I had limited

16

expectations; it took me two years to get into this class. I'm appreciative of the course since it provides for those who can't read." All of the students enjoy the courses offered by Ms. Williams and see this as a means of fitting into Bermuda society.

Chief Officer Mr. Hubert Dean said: "The classes are available for those who need it. I wish she was here every day, but she had to be shared." This year's graduation class promises to be the biggest graduating class to-date. The inmates are screened and processed by Ms. Williams on their education level, which determines the class best suited for them.

Another student said: "This is my first time here, and some of the younger guys that come in need help. I'm from the hotel field and can handle people. I got caught up and I can accept that, but I can apply what I have learned when I'm released." A 43-year-old GED graduate said: "When I came in, I had a fourth grade education. I got my diploma, and I'm studying for a college degree. Education is not a priority, and that's why prisons are the way they are. I used my incarceration to my advantage. I never had an interest in education, but now I'm more educationally inclined, and learning is the key."

The inmates are hoping for an expansion of the computer learning programme to meet the increasing demand for Ms. William's tutoring.

# HOPE TIME FOR YOUNG OFFENDERS

## 1987

The original idea behind the prison was that it would provide young offenders with the opportunity for solitary repentance and, finally, rehabilitation.

A period of corrective training has several distinct functions:

- To punish the crime

- To deter others who might be tempted to commit the crime themselves

- To remove the offenders from society

- To rehabilitate the offender

- To give the offender the attitudes and skills that will enable them to take up a law-abiding life on release

The Co-Ed detention facility in St. George's has been dubbed "the salvage point for young offenders," whose crimes range from breaching probation to allowing a dog attack on a Police officer.

Some of the inmates realize that while they are paying their debt to society, the stigma of their incarceration may linger for some time.

All the trainees agree that being deprived of their freedom has allowed them to reflect upon mistakes made in the past.

Personal experiences are put into music, turned into plays or anything that will warn others that life in the fast lane is not always the best.

The fleeting illusion for one trainee is that publication of her material will have to wait until her release. "That can be anywhere between nine months and three years," she said.

One 20-year-old trainee said: "I'm a slow worker and suffer from epilepsy which stopped me from progressing. It made me frustrated, and I breached my probation, but now I regret it. I have a special class on Thursday and Ms. (Neletha) Williams is willing to help me when I get out. I've been here a year and a half; I hope to go abroad once I leave and work with social assistance. That way, I can deter kids from making some of the same mistakes that I have made."

One 20-year-old student who is in the remedial reading class said: "I'm learning a lot since

I've been here. The only thing that is missing is my GED (high school diploma). This is a time when I can catch myself, and carpentry is my trade. We do work for schools, like the shelves, and that way I feel like I am putting something back into society." He says his downfall stemmed from being in the wrong clique and wanting to grow up too soon.

A 19-year-old remedial student said: "Since I've been here, I've improved a lot. My reading was poor. I would have been worse had I been on the outside. Before, I couldn't take in a pair of pants, now I make clothes. Fashion design is what's on my mind."

Family ties are strengthened through day release programmes and visitation, but a 30-year-old inmate said: "I left school early, lived like a rebel and followed the crowd. While I'm here, I have the opportunity to accomplish something. I have a five-year-old daughter and, if one doesn't set a good example, it will reflect upon the children." She said: "It's hard for me to be away from her for so long. Drugs were what landed me here and I don't let her see me. I've been in this predicament before, and she may not understand fully, but she has a basic idea of my incarceration."

The drama outlet allowed one trainee to write three plays from personal experiences, which serve as a warning for wayward children. Career choices range from lab technicians to architecture, and Chief Officer Mr. Roland Pearman praised the trainees for their interest in the vocational and academic courses that are offered at the facility. Mr. Pearman said: "We used to have classes five mornings a week, and I'm striving to have that again. Education is a good foundation for the future, which plays a good part in reforming them." Once reunited with their families, the trainees hope that their material will be published and that their reform will help them become better role models for the younger members of their families.

# GRADUATION CLASS OF 1987 – CASEMATES PRISON

21ˢᵗ November, 1987

*"I wish to congratulate you all on your recent achievements.*
*By graduating at this time you have shown that through*
*hard work and determination you can excel.*
*It is my hope that you will continue in this positive vein*
*throughout your lives."*

**L. Frederick Wade, J.P., M.P. – Opposition Leader**

The 1987 graduation was held at the Prison Officer's Club where nine inmates received their GED (high school diploma certificate). The guest speaker was Dr. Rev. Vernon G. Lambe Sr. In attendance were graduates' families, students of the GED and Computer Class who assisted in the programme, and Mrs. Solange Saltus from the Bermuda College who presented the graduating students with their CLEP Examination results, and the prison administration.

**Graduates Pledge**

*"Real opportunity or success lies within the person and not the job; you can best get to the top by getting to the bottom of things."*

The rewards of application and dedication were never more evident to me, than during this past year. As I watched some of my fellow inmates under the guidance of Ms. Butterfield study and aspire to reach new heights. Some of them successfully achieved their goal, and we gather here tonight to pay tribute to them, but to those who tried and were unsuccessful, full credit is due to you for your valiant effort. One reason many people never attempt new things is their fear of failure, but you can go where you want to go, do what you want to do, have what you want to have, and be what you want to be if you continue to make the effort.

We, the graduates of the Class of '87, hereby pledge to continue our quest to obtain knowledge, improve our abilities and to renew our convictions to strive for a better life for ourselves, our families and our fellowmen.

We thank you Ms. Williams Butterfield for your inspiration, dedication, and concern, and we pledge to uphold the standards of excellence, loyalty, honesty, and integrity which you have given us through your kind and caring ways.

*"Knowledge has to be improved, challenged and increased constantly or it vanishes."*

**By Stephen Cann – Graduate 1987**

**Graduates of 1987 Class**

Leo Lewis

Milton Watson

Stephen Cann

Michael Ebbin

Curtis Dearing

Colin Lee

Marco Puga

Hubert Rogers

Oliver Simmons

## Educational Officer's Message

This occasion of the third Annual Graduation of the students at Casemates Prisons is the realization of a 15-year-old dream. This is just an example of what can be achieved when there is a combination of a caring administration, a dedicated teacher like Ms. Butterfield, and students who are prepared to make themselves available to take advantage of the opportunities as they occur.

It has been wisely stated in the Bible that "without a vision the people will perish." This vision of the Educational Department is for the system to provide programmes which would allow each inmate some opportunity to improve his basic academic readiness.

My sincere thanks to Ms. Butterfield for her dedication and unselfish service. If we had two like her, we would be in excellent shape.

Congratulations to the 1987 graduates. You have reached the first steps of your dream. May you be inspired to move onward and upward.

To all assembled here tonight, may the joy of Christmas and the love of God be with you and throughout the year ahead.

**Mr. Edwin Wilson – Educational Officer**

## Instructor's Message

Sincere congratulations to you, the graduates of the Class of '87. This evening ceremony symbolizes the joy and success which you are experiencing. I ask that you continue your education development, being careful to learn from others, making sure that you teach yourself. Be industrious and cultivate your own self-esteem. May your continuing efforts bring greater success to each one of you and profit the community in which you choose to live and work.

I am thankful to God for inspiring me to be of assistance to you, and my prayer is that your accomplishments have provided that solid foundation that you would need in order to meet life's challenges with confidence and strength.

Remember that education is the key to survival skills, knowledge and understanding. The key to happiness is having dreams and the key to success is making them come true.

**Neletha Butterfield – GED Instructor/Computer Consultant**

# GRADUATION CLASS OF 1987 – PRISON FARM AND CO-ED

25th November, 1987

*"We are the world, learning, love, peace, happiness, unity, wisdom and knowledge, for learning is the Key to Success"*

**—Co-Ed Facility Class of '87**

The third Annual Graduation was held at the Co-Ed Correctional Facility for both the Prison Farm and Co-Ed students of the GED class. The guest speaker was Mr. Dale Butler, and the ceremony was attended by family, friends, and prison administration. Students and graduates participated in the programme as the master of ceremonies, welcome, musical selections, and a vote of thanks. Several inmates received their GED (high school diploma).

**Graduating Class of 1987**

Copeland
Stanley
Christopher

**Instructor's Message**

Sincere congratulations to you the graduates of the Class of '87. This evening ceremony symbolizes the joy and success which you are experiencing. I ask, that you continue your education development, being careful to learn from others, making sure that you teach yourself. Be industrious and cultivate your own self-esteem. May your continuing efforts bring greater success to each one of you and profit the community in which you choose to live and work.

I am thankful to God for inspiring me to be of assistance to you and my prayer is that your accomplishments have provided that solid foundation that you would need in order to meet life's challenges with confidence and strength.

Remember that education is the key to survival skills, knowledge and understanding. The key to happiness is having dreams and the key to success is making them come true.

**–Neletha Butterfield – GED Instructor /Computer Consultant**

## Office Of The Opposition Leader

FRONT STREET, HAMILTON 5-24, BERMUDA TELEPHONE: 809(29)2-2665

November 21, 1987.

The Graduates,
Class of 1987,
Casemates Prisons,
Sandy's.

Dear Sirs,

On behalf of the Bermuda Progressive Labour Party I wish to congratulate you all on your recent achievements. By graduating at this time you have shown that with hard work and determination you can excel. It is my hope that you will continue in this positive vein throughout your lives.

Unfortunately I am unable to be with you at this time to extend my personal congratulations as our Party is hosting our Annual Conference Banquet tonight.

Once again, I say congratulations and may I encourage you to press on with your academic endeavours.

Sincerely,

L. Frederick Wade, J.P., M.P.
Opposition Leader (and)
Leader of the Bermuda
Progressive Labour Party

LFW:ic

# MINISTRY OF HEALTH AND SOCIAL SERVICES

P.O. Box HM 380
Hamilton  HM BX
Bermuda
Telephone: (809) 236-0224

11th May, 1989

TO WHOM IT MAY CONCERN
-------------------------

## Ms. Neletha Butterfield

I have recently made the acquaintance of Ms. Butterfield, but have had the opportunity to familiarise myself with the educational programmes she offers to Prisons.

I am most impressed with the ranges of subjects she offers, the level of participation of prisoners and her success with the G.E.D. programme and computer literacy programmes.

Her method of using computers to assist with teaching is not new, but they have had a very dramatic impact on the educational programmes in Prisons.

Her programmes have my support and I would agree to any assistance which would further enhance the education of persons incarcerated.

Yours sincerely,

Hon. Quinton L. Edness
Minister of Health, Social
Services and Housing
-----------------------------

ELD/sf

# LETTER ON REHABILITATION IN PRISON

2ⁿᵈ March, 1988

*"You can give rehabilitation and provide all the opportunities to start life over, but unless that person changes his heart, he hasn't changed anything."*

**—CPB (Volunteer) – Smith's Parish**

Dear Sir,

One of the main reasons why our prison population has grown tremendously over the last 10 years is due to repeat offenders.

Taken from a mandate on international figures of prisons the priorities of the running of prisons are first to control and separate the prison population from society, second to ensure safety within the prison and thirdly rehabilitation if possible.

To prevent the prison populations growing further and hopefully to decrease it in the future, the goal of a number of volunteers is to assist the Prison Administration in placing rehabilitation on an equal footing as security.

Worldwide statistics of prison populations reveal that broken homes and poor education are the two most significant reasons why people end up in prison.

There is not much we can do about the broken homes but there is something we can do about improving education of inmates whilst incarcerated.

First, Roots Assembly an arts and crafts exhibition took place in November 1987. It was an event inspired, created, and organized by the inmates with the encouragement of the Prison Administration and a number of volunteers. The sculptures, paintings and carpentry were viewed by hundreds of people from the public who expressed amazement at the artistic and professional works produced by the inmates. Support also came from Mr. Harry Soares, Member of Parliament, who was the patron of Roots Assembly, and a number of financial contributions were received also from organisations such as the Lions Club, the Bermuda Commercial Bank and the Kiwanis Club.

Roots Assembly could not have been possible without Mr. Trott who teaches sculpture classes at Casemates a number of times a week and has done so for many years.

**Neletha Williams,** also a volunteer, who teaches computer programmes to inmates, had a display at Roots Assembly showing the types of computers used by the inmates and some of their work. This brought the public's attention the other types of education taught and made them aware that there is great potential for expanding due to the avid interest of a number of inmates in all of Bermuda's Prisons.

The most recent events taking place at Casemates have been the intercell block Quiz Competitions that were the brainchild of Mr. Jack Harris (volunteer) and have brought much excitement, competitiveness, and a lot of thinking among the inmates.

The Quiz questions are comprised primarily of Bermudian history, geography, sports, and general knowledge similar to Round the Rock.

After a number of these Quiz Competitions took place between the different cells, the overall winners were Cell Block 4.

Again, using international figures, the average person has to make hundreds of decisions a day; however, due to the regimented life of the prison system, the average inmate makes only thirty-six decisions a day. Obviously, these quizzes are a good educational stimulant for the inmates.

As a result of the inmates' intense interest, a team of the best qualifiers was chosen to play against the Lions Club. One of the purposes of the Quiz was to give members of the public and the inmates the chance to meet each other in a positive light.

On 10th February, 1988, a beautiful silver cup was presented to the winning Cell Block by Harry Soares, M.P., at the Casemates Prison. Also, at this time, Mr. Neville Tatem Jr. donated to Casemates library a set of encyclopedias on behalf of his publishers. They were received by a very happy head librarian, an inmate.

Then the Quiz kicked off at 7:00 p.m. between the Lions Club Team and the Inmates Team at Casemates. For one hour, I could hardly contain my excitement as there was almost a tie all the way until the last decisive winning question, which the inmates won!

Seeing the inmates' elation at winning the Quiz and the enjoyment shown by the Lions Club members inspired me to let the public know of the positive events taking place in our prisons.

First, a thank you to the Lions Club for participating in the Quiz; congratulations to the present Prison Administration for their forward thinking and encouragement, and a big congratulations to the winning Inmates Team.

In ending, I would like to repeat a very important aspect of rehabilitation expressed to me by a reformed inmate.

"You can give rehabilitation and provide all the opportunities to start life over, but unless that person changes his heart, he hasn't changed anything."

The goals of the volunteers are to provide the opportunity to change the heart.

**CPB (Volunteer)**
**Smith's Parish**

(Letter to the editor of *The Royal Gazette*)

# LETTER FROM INMATE REQUESTING CLASSES

8ᵗʰ March, 1988

*"We believe that when people make mistakes*
*They deserve the opportunity to remake their lives."*

**—President Barack Obama**

Dear Miss Williams,

I hope this letter finds you in the best of health. I have been trying to get in contact with you for quite some time now and all my attempts have been fruitless. So now I have taken the opportunity to write you to see if you can get any satisfaction with my request. As you know when I first come into this establishment you had me doing an aptitude course to evaluate my academic stability. However it's not just been weeks but months since you have abandoned and deserted me. I have made every effort to get the Prison Administration to get in contact with you so I can enhance my education and apply myself to some serious educational courses. However, I have come to the conclusion that as long as this Administration sees an inmate striving to attain the goals he has set before him regardless of the misfortunes his had in life they don't seem to cooperate. As long as they could keep us blacks illiterate and enhancing ourselves they seem happy. I appeal to you through this letter to arrange a day to come and see me so I can get started on some courses. You have evaluated my academic standard what conclusion you have come to I don't know. However I am tired of lingering I want to apply myself to something more constructive and attain the goals I have set. I appreciate you taking the time to read this letter. I hope your decision will be beneficial to me.

Sincerely yours,
Inmate S. Archibald
P.S. Thanks for the Christmas candy.

# EXCEEDING YOUR EXPECTATION THROUGH EDUCATION IN THE PRISON

Presented by:
Neletha Butterfield
Computer Assisted Instruction Consultant
Friday, 20th May, 1988

## EXCEEDING YOUR EXPECTATIONS THROUGH EDUCATION

Exceeding your expectations through EDUCATION means that you should go beyond what is expected of you. Through the educational process, you can expect to have a future and strive for excellence and success.

**TO EDUCATE MEANS:** To provide schooling, to teach; to train mentally and morally; to improve and to develop. EDUCATION is a lifetime process, a process through:

**INFANCY:** A complete dependence on others, the nourishing and nurturing process.

**CHILDHOOD:** Taking our first steps; a process from which we have just emerged.

**ADOLESCENCE:** A process of growing up, with new and most accepting challenges.

**ADULTHOOD:** The stage of full and complete responsibility of our needs and efforts.

Through this educational process, strive for expectations, excellence, and success. Success is the progressive realization of a dream. It will open doors in so many areas that have been closed to you in the past. Allow us to share our knowledge that education can enable us to "EXCEED OUR EXPECTATIONS."

A guide to assist you in improving your awareness to EDUCATION, utilizing the word: **E D U C A T I O N**

E – **ENHANCING:** To enhance; to make students recognize that they are great and they can be greater.

**ENCOURAGE:** To give help. Encouragement is necessary even more so in the prisons, where inmates feel a sense of rejection.

**EXCITING:** Learning is fun. When we are excited, we are open to receive and retrieve valuable information.

D – **DARE:** Dare to try to exceed, to be educated. Dare to be different. Dare to be determined to make a decision and a commitment.

**DISCIPLINE:** You must be disciplined, gaining self-control, conduct and accepting the system of rules.

U – **UNDERSTAND:** Understand the need for EDUCATION.

**UNLOCK:** Unlock some human values you have never experienced before—*faith, hope* and *love*. These values can be the driving force propelling you to success.

C – **COMMIT:** Commit yourself to EXCEED. Enroll in a class; take a course. If you fail, at least you have the pride of knowing you have conquered the fear of failure.

**CONFIDENCE:** Have confidence in yourself that you can do better, and you will achieve.

A – **ATTITUDE:** The number one key factor in learning. Your attitude must be conducive to learning, if you want to do better. It is no good trying to achieve a goal if your attitude or behavior is not at its best.

**AFFIRM:** Affirm that you can do it and have the ability to find a job. You can change careers; you can recover and not spend the rest of your life in prison. You can learn to read; for reading is the key to learning everything else.

T – **TRY:** Attempt, endeavour. To try is to risk failure; risk must be taken because the greatest hazard in life is to risk nothing.

**TIME:** Use it wisely. With the time you have available, increase your knowledge. Don't let the TIME serve you; you serve the time.

**TOOLS:** Your tools are important. During classes, make sure you have your tools. A student coming to class without his TOOLS is a person going to his job not prepared to work.

I – **INTEREST:** Show interest in yourself, your family, and your educational skills.

**IMAGINE:** Imagine how you can accomplish your goals through the educational process.

**IMPROVE:** Improve yourselves in order to improve mankind.

**ILLITERACY:** There is a high percentage of illiteracy within the prisons. In order to cure this problem, we must go "BACK TO BASICS." Basic skills, basic values, and basic discipline; remember that those afflicted with illiteracy are keen to learn, but too much pride steps in the way. A sense of INSECURITY can be cured; learn how to read. Reading opens a new world. It is a good feeling just knowing you know.

O – **OVERLOOK:** Overlook your obstacles and face your problems. To overcome them, you have to manage them.

**OPPORTUNITIES:** A good chance of upward mobility awaits you. Once we have a high school education and more, we must stop accepting jobs that do not give us any upward mobility. Too many of us get satisfied with the menial work. Through higher educational skills, better opportunities in the job field await us.

N – **NEVER:** Never accept defeat. Believe that somehow, somewhere, sometime, through someone's help, you can achieve your heart's highest goal. You can make it happen somewhere—though not necessarily where you are today.

# ADULT EDUCATION

| ADULT SKILLS | ADULT MATH SKILLS | ADULT READING SKILLS | | ADULT LANGUAGE SKILLS |
|---|---|---|---|---|
| **GED COURSES** | GED | GED | GED | GED | GED |
| **HIGH SCHOOL DIPLOMA** | MATH | LITERATURE | SCIENCE | SOCIAL STUDIES | ENGLISH |

# COLLEGE LEVEL EXAMINATION PREPARATION
# (C.L.E.P.)

# CORRESPONDENCE COURSES

NEW YORK INSTITUTE OF TECHNOLOGY

PENN STATE UNIVERSITY

The correspondence courses will enable you to work towards a Bachelor of Science or

Bachelor of Arts degree in various areas, for example: Business Administration, Art, Behavioral Science, and more.

# COMPUTER COURSES

COMPUTER LITERACY

INTRODUCTION TO COMPUTERS

and

PROGRAMMING

WORD PROCESSING

COMPUTERIZED ACCOUNTING

The mentioned courses are available to you in the prisons in addition to remedial classes in reading, math and English. On your release, you can continue your studies at the Bermuda College, Devonshire or at C.A.R.E. Computer School, a private school specializing in higher education. In closing, let me conclude that no matter what your problem is—illiteracy, math, or higher education—somehow, somewhere, someway, sometime, there is someone who has the key to wisdom to set you free.

# MY FUTURE IS MY RESPONSIBILITY

20th May, 1988
Casemates Prison

*Addiction Services presented a Community Resource Workshop held at Casemates Prison in the chapel from 16th May – 20th May, 1988. The following presentation by Neletha Butterfield on* **EDUCATION** *was noted by inmate Mervin C. E. Curtis in "An Inmates Perspective"*

Our last night was very good in every way you can put it. Our opening prayer was taken by brother Raymond Grant. Then Mr. Russ Ford introduced Brother Outta Sight Simmons. Brother Simmons along with music from Brother Ebbin on the piano did a very good introduction of Miss Butterfield our guest speaker of the night. Miss Butterfield of C.A.R.E. Computer School explained everything to us about education and computers and the word "Education" means a lot. She went on to explain each and every letter in the word. She also told us education is a must, not just in prison, but also outside. In prison, it can get one ready for when he or she leaves to get a job or to carry on their education as far as college abroad. Miss Butterfield then introduced Brother Calvin Richardson. She said it was not easy with him, but he has made it; that's great! Brother Richardson gave us a short speech on how he has made out so far in class and thanked Miss Butterfield for pushing him because without her, he would not have made it. He also in so many words told us to join up.

Miss Butterfield then introduced Brother Ebbin who is in a higher stage in the class. Brother Ebbin told us straightforward about himself coming out in the class. He thought he had it all when he came in here until the schooling came. Now he is about to go on to another level in the computer class. He thanked Miss Butterfield very much indeed and also told us a few things. We have to get ourselves some education. She then introduced Brother Raymond Grant. Brother Grant who is also in the computer class enlightened us even more; he told us just as Brother Ebbin, and now the brother is doing courses in college abroad to gain a degree in Art, I mean a Bachelor's Degree. He then thanked Miss Butterfield and pointed out to us "Our Future is Our Responsibility," so get hip and join. Miss Butterfield introduced her last speaker, Brother Shane. Shane told us in doing time in Casemates, he joined the computer class which helped him a lot in getting out of prison; he is now a foreman on a job in charge of 13 people and has a new outlook on life.

All thanks to Miss Butterfield again; she has and still is doing a great job for lots of inmates in our prisons. I have signed up for her classes so I can better my education and help myself better in life as well as others. Our night continued with Mr. Russ Ford introducing Mr. Llewellyn Gomes of Addiction Services. Mr. Gomes along with Mr. David Brangman, once a drug abuser as well as Brother Grant, Brother K. Martin, and Brother C. Johnson gave us a therapeutic exercise which was very good for me. It shows where one is true about his or her feelings, and they opened up expressing everything. I would like to take part in one; it is good therapy for anyone, and it really helps. Mr. Gomes got a good round of applause.

Mr. Russ Ford introduced our former Commissioner Mr. Edward Dyer. Mr. Dyer went on to praise Miss Butterfield and Mr. Ford and company for the Workshop, hoping that all attendees gained from it and will do better in life. Keep in mind, "Your Future Is Your Responsibility." Mr. Milton Pringle our Acting Commissioner came next. He thanked one and all and said he had had a lot of feedback about this Workshop from his officers, who really enjoyed it and would love very much to have one for them. Mr. Pringle said it's good because for years, he and others were trying to get people like Johnson and others to help themselves; it's a very big step which each and every one should take. Then our Acting Chief, Mr. Calvin Hollis, went on to tell us he thinks the Workshop is good for everyone but reminded us to keep in mind, "My Future Is My Responsibility."

My personal feeling for this whole week of the Community Resource Workshop was a week I'll never forget. It has really made me look and think about life in different ways. We have had a whole week of speakers coming to us from all different departments telling us true facts of our future and our responsibility.

# EVERYBODY

EVERYBODY is moving and nobody's going anywhere

EVERYBODY loves you, but no one cares

EVERYBODY is your friend, but when needed they're never there

EVERYBODY is groovin and it's to the wrong song

EVERYBODY is right no-one wants to admit they're wrong

EVERYBODY is smoking, nobody is getting high

     So many on the ground, trying to live in the sky

EVERYBODY feels strong to know that another is weak

     All our mistakes, wrong doings and faults in life they seek

EVERYBODY is talking and not really saying a thing

EVERYBODY is complaining about the system but no-one takes a stand

EVERYBODY is concerned about the children

     No one reaches out to take their hand

     The adults today are just a bunch of children

     Proclaiming to be women and men

EVERYBODY has a theory of life that we do not understand

EVERYBODY is fighting and the good LORD knows it's for the wrong cause

We think we know ourselves, but a lot of us are lost

Before we wake-up and say hello to life, it's passed you by

So, instead of saying hello you're saying bye, bye.


Written by
Nyal Saunders
PRISON FARM
November 1998


May God bless all who read this poem during my time of incarceration. (Given to my caring teacher Ms. Neletha Butterfield on 4th November, 1988 with love and thanks).

# PRISON APPOINTMENT LOOKS WRONG – PLP

17th November, 1988

A plum teaching position in the prison system has been awarded to Mrs. Nadine Lapsley-Dyer whose husband, Mr. Edward Dyer, is Permanent secretary for Health and Social Services, the department which runs the prison system.

But Mrs. Lapsley-Dyer yesterday defended her qualifications for the position, saying her husband's position in no way helped her win the $43,000 posting.

"I was teaching in the prison system before I met my husband," said Mrs. Lapsley-Dyer, who holds a master's degree in special education from Washington, DC's Howard University and who taught in the prison system in both 1978 and 1983. She added, "I also expected people to talk—that's the norm in a position like this. I guess I'm not surprised that people think I can't get a job based on my own qualifications."

Mrs. Lapsley-Dyer, currently a child development specialist at the Child Development Project at Tynes Bay House, was named to the post after a rigorous screening process which ended with the Public Service Commission approving the recommendation made by a panel of prison system professionals. Mrs. Lapsley-Dyer won the position over a field of applicants, which included prison education supporter Ms. Neletha Butterfield, whose work over the past four years has helped 39 inmates obtain their high school graduation certificates and Mrs. Veronica Mitchell, who has taught in the prison system for the last three years. Mrs. Mitchell, who holds a Bachelor of Education degree from the City University of New York and now teaches at Devonshire Academy, was shocked to hear of the decision. "It sounds like a political appointment to me," Mrs. Mitchell said. "I thought I had a good chance at the job, based on my experience. That's a very interesting appointment."

It's the suggestion of nepotism that angers people, Mr. Wade said. "It just looks wrong; justice doesn't appear to have been done," Mr. Wade said. "It looks like Mr. Dyer recommended his wife for the job, which is wrong."

But Mr. Dyer said he had nothing to do with the appointment: "Other than being aware of her application for the position and then hearing from her last week that she had been chosen, I had nothing to do with it," he said, and Health and Social Services Minister the Hon. Quinton Edness said he was satisfied that Mr. Dyer's position did not affect the selection process. "I'm satisfied that it was handled in a very professional manner, and that any claims of nepotism are unfounded," Mr. Edness said.

# SMART INMATES

Prisoners are excelling in a new field of endeavor—education.

In a graduation ceremony at the Prison Officers' Recreation Club last weekend, 12 Casemates prisoners received their high school diplomas. On Wednesday, two inmates from the Prison Farm and one from the Co-ed facility at Ferry Reach also received their GED, or general certificate of education.

Neletha Williams, the person who provided the means for these inmates to complete their high-school education while in prison, is extremely pleased with the achievements for students have made.

"This is the third graduation we've had," she said. "A total of 35 inmates have received their diplomas since 1985."

Using computer as a teaching aid, Ms. Williams has coached the inmates in reading and writing skills, math, social studies, and science.

She owns her own business called CARE (Children and Adults Reaching for Education) and, outside her work every day in the prisons, she has 70 students enrolled in her evening tutorial programmes in the basement of her Pembroke home.

Nine of the 35 who received their high-school diplomas over the last two years are now working on college-level exams with the assistance of the Bermuda College.

A total of 123 inmates have been introduced to the world of computers since 1984, and 19 have been substantially helped with their reading skills. Two, said Ms. Williams learned to read for the first time.

```
GRADUATES PLEDGE
****************
```

    We, the graduating class of 1988, would like to thank
you for encouraging us to hold on - to hold on to a vision
that has become a reality today. For some of us it was a
period of revision and for some, a period of completion, but
we held on. Somewhere out there, saints were upholding
Burnell, Yusef, Kay-Marie and myself in effectual and
fervent prayer. Today is proof of the answer to those
prayers.
    On behalf of the graduating class, I say a big "Thank
You" and "God Bless You" to our family, our friends, our
loved ones and all those who encouraged us to stay in the
race. Graduation Day or Moving On Day is special to us and
thank you all for sharing with us in our joy of
accomplishments.

God Bless You.

Phyllis Burchall  -  Graduate 1988

```
GRADUATES
*********

Phyllis Burchall
Yusef DeSilva
Burnell Hill
Kay-Marie Lewis
```

```
Programme:    C.A.R.E. Computer Services
Front Cover:  Stevon Somersall
```

We Are The World

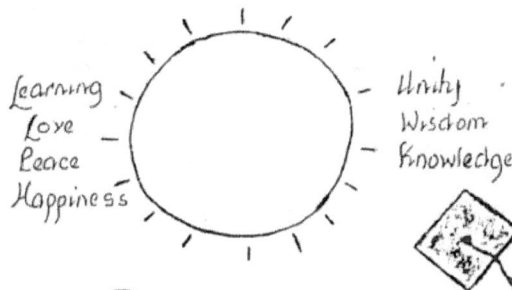

Learning
Love
Peace
Happiness

Unity
Wisdom
Knowledge

Learning is the key to Success

Co-ed Facility & Prison Farm

3rd ANNUAL GRADUATION & PRIZEGIVING
8th OCTOBER, 1988

| | |
|---|---|
| Master of Ceremonies | Eusi Wainwright (G.E.D. Student) |
| Processional | GRADUATES |
| Opening Hymn | "Walking the Light" |
| Opening Prayer | Carla Johnson |
| Scripture | Arlene Eddy |
| Welcome | Stevon Somersall |
| Selection | "Element" |
| Introduction of Speaker | Ms. Neletha Butterfield |
| Selection | Co-Ed Choir |

SPEAKER: Rev. Silvester Beaman

***** Presentation of Certificates & Awards *****

| | |
|---|---|
| Selection | "Element" |
| GRADUATES PLEDGE | Phyllis Burchall |

****** GRADUATES PARTICIPATION ******

| | |
|---|---|
| Remarks | Ms. Neletha Butterfield G.E.D. Instructor |
| Remarks | Mr. Allen Richardson Acting Educ. Officer |
| Selection | Co-Ed Choir |
| Vote of Thanks | Kay-Marie Lewis |
| Closing Remarks | Chief Officer Lambert |
| Closing Prayer | Rev. Silvester Beaman |
| Recessional | I'll Be Alright |

INSTRUCTOR'S MESSAGE
***********************

Sincere congratulations to you, the graduates of the CLASS OF '88. This evening's ceremony symbolizes the joy and success which you are experiencing. I ask, that you continue your educational development, being careful to learn from others and making sure that you teach yourself. Be industrious and cultivate your own self-esteem. May your continuing efforts bring greater success to each one of you and profit the community in which you choose to live and work.

I am thankful to God for inspiring me to be of assistance to you and my prayer is that your accomplishments have provided that solid foundation that you will need in order to meet life's challenges with confidence and strength. It has been wisely stated in the Bible that "without a vision the people perish." This vision of the Educational Department is for the system to provide programmes which would allow each inmate some opportunity to improve his/her basic academic readiness.

Remember that education is the key to survival skills, knowledge and understanding. The key to happiness is having dreams and the key to success is making them come true. My sincere thanks to the Prison Administration and to all assembled here tonight, may the love of God be with you.

Neletha Butterfield
G.E.D. Instructor/Computer Consultant

# EDITORIAL: APPLAUD PRISONERS' GRADUATION

The recent prisoners' graduation at Casemates represents the approach toward rehabilitation which should be encouraged.

Too often Bermuda's criminal justice system has emphasized treating the symptoms of antisocial behaviour instead of examining the root causes.

Our prisons, which are overwhelmingly populated with young, black men, have historically been a dead-end street. After serving time, ex-prisoners have a monumental task of getting integrated back into society. The combination of inadequate marketable skills and the unwillingness of many merchants to take a chance often leads the young offender back to the very company of people that he might be trying to avoid.

Achieving educational goals and expressing creativity builds self-esteem which social scientists generally point to as being crucial to rehabilitation.

When these graduates and other certificate winners are released, society also needs to be ready to give them the chance to develop their full potential.

We should applaud the efforts of Government, volunteer teachers, parents, relatives and friends of the prisoners, and the prisoners most of all, for making such a graduation possible.

20th June, 1990

Hon D. Neletha Butterfield, M.B.E., J.P.

# MINISTRY OF HEALTH AND SOCIAL SERVICES

P.O. Box HM 380
Hamilton HM BX
Bermuda
Telephone: (809) 236-0224

11th May, 1989

TO WHOM IT MAY CONCERN
------------------------

### Ms. Neletha Butterfield

I have recently made the acquaintance of Ms. Butterfield, but have had the opportunity to familiarise myself with the educational programmes she offers to Prisons.

I am most impressed with the ranges of subjects she offers, the level of participation of prisoners and her success with the G.E.D. programme and computer literacy programmes.

Her method of using computers to assist with teaching is not new, but they have had a very dramatic impact on the educational programmes in Prisons.

Her programmes have my support and I would agree to any assistance which would further enhance the education of persons incarcerated.

Yours sincerely,

Hon. Quinton L. Edness
Minister of Health, Social
Services and Housing
-----------------------------

ELD/sf

42

**THE MINISTRY OF EDUCATION AND CULTURE**
Office of The Minister

7 POINT FINGER ROAD, PAGET, BERMUDA
MAILING ADDRESS: P.O. BOX HM 1185, HAMILTON HM EX, BERMUDA
TELEPHONE: (809) 236-6904   FAX: (809) 236-4006

REFERENCE NO.

4-5-26(a)

To Whom It May Concern,

The computer education programme which is conducted by Ms. Neletha Butterfield at the Coed Facility and at Casemates has been visited by staff of the Department of Education who have reported the following:

Computers are used for the following purposes:

1.   tutoring - teaching and reinforcing skills outlined in the GED programme

2.   remediation - upgrading basic skills of inmates

3.   enrichment - instruction in programming

Staff have reported the need for the upgrading of the equipment in order to improve the programme. They have reported also that they have been asked to assist in recommending suitable hardware and software. Their report has included also the observation on the rapport which exists between Ms. Butterfield and the inmates who speak highly of the positive influence which she has had on their lives.

Marion Robinson, Ph.D.
Permanent Secretary

MR/sh

cc: Permanent Secretary, Health and Social Services

Striving Towards Excellence
Every Child A Winner

Hon D. Neletha Butterfield, M.B.E., J.P.

*Treatment of Offenders Commissioners*

*Hamilton, Bermuda*

10th February, 1989

Ms. Neletha Butterfield
c/o Prisons Department
Prison Headquarters
Happy Valley Rd.,
Pembroke.

Dear Ms. Butterfield:

The Treatment of Offenders Board extend their appreciation to you
for a great job you are doing in the Prisons.  The Board wishes
you every success and congratulates you on the recent graduation.

Yours faithfully,

Secretary
Treatment of Offenders Board

# GED/COMPUTER PROGRAMME: CO-EDUCATIONAL FACILITY

## FERRY REACH, ST. GEORGE'S

**HOURS OF OPERATION:** Mondays   9:30 a.m. – 11:30 a.m.

                                     Thursdays  9:30 a.m. – 11:30 a.m.

## GENERAL EDUCATION DEVELOPMENT (GED) PROGRAMME

The General Educational Development (GED) programme is to assist each student (trainees/inmates) in obtaining their high school equivalency diploma. Students are orally instructed in five area, utilizing GED textbooks (provided by prisons). The areas are as follows:

**SOCIAL STUDIES:** Students read and interpret graphs and charts. Selections are from the area of U.S. history, economics, sociology, political science, government, current affairs, geography, anthropology and Bermuda history.

**SCIENCE:** Students study and answer questions to the basic science concepts. They are able to interpret illustrations and read passages, being able to show that they can understand what they have read. Apply the information to a new situation, analyze relationships among ideas and make judgements about the material being presented. **Areas:** biology, life sciences, physical sciences, earth science, chemistry and physics.

**READING SKILLS:** Focuses on reading skills. These skills are called comprehension, application, analysis, synthesis and evaluation. The skills mentioned are like layers of a pyramid. Each higher level skill rests on the skill that precedes it. One skill is a stepping stone to a higher one. Knowledge (memory) is the foundation of the pyramid. At the memory level they will recall the facts.

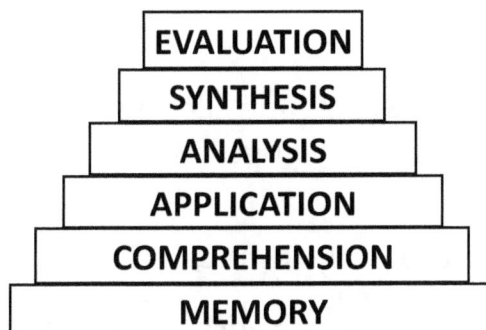

| EVALUATION |
| :---: |
| SYNTHESIS |
| ANALYSIS |
| APPLICATION |
| COMPREHENSION |
| MEMORY |

**WRITING SKILLS: PART I and PART II.** In Part I, students are instructed in the area of sentence structure, grammar and usage, punctuation, spelling and capitalization. In Part II, Essay writing, students are given general knowledge topics to write about. They should be able to plan, organize their thinking on an issue and be able to communicate thoughts clearly on paper. Assisted in the areas of spelling, punctuation and sentence, writing skills.

**MATHEMATICS:** Students practice in basic math skills, as well as crucial problem solving. The areas covered are: arithmetic, algebra, geometry, fractions and decimals. Students are constantly practicing and being tested bi-weekly on the area already covered during a math session.

## COMPUTER PROGRAMME

Presently, C.A.R.E. Computer Services has installed four (4) computer terminals in the classroom at the Co-Educational Facility. Since January 1989, the operation of this programme is costing C.A.R.E. $350.00 monthly. (*In urgent need of a sponsor, prison assistance or funds to keep this programme operational). Each student (Trainee/inmate) enrolled in the class receives a minimum of thirty (30) minutes of computer instruction on the days stated. This programme also reinforces the oral work given for the GED preparation. The areas of computer instruction are as follows:

Problem Solving

Math

Geometry, Statistics, Functions, Sets

Algebra

Reading Skills

Critical Reading Skills

Fundamentals of English

Computer Literacy

Most of the courses available on the computer allow ten (10) minutes of instruction. (Can be adjusted, but time is limited). Brief descriptions of the courses are as follows:

## PROBLEM SOLVING: (4 years of daily instruction)

Provides instruction and practice in the practical mathematical thinking skills needed to solve seven content areas: How Many, Money, Mystery Numbers and Age, Measurements, Number Systems and Time, Rate and Distance.

**MATH SKILLS**: (8 years of daily instruction)

Provides exercises in twelve (12) comprehensive mathematic strands: Addition, Subtraction, Multiplication, Division, Number Concepts, Equations, U.S. Measurements, Metric Measurements, Fractions, Decimals, Applications and Problem Solving.

**GEOMETRY, STATISTICS, FUNCTIONS, ETC**. (1 year daily instruction)

Provides instruction in important areas of secondary mathematics. Example: triangles, squares, number lines, octagons, curves, circles, graphs and charts.

**ALGEBRA**: (1 year of daily instruction)

Teaches basic algebraic concepts and techniques for solving equations.

**READING**: (4.5 years of daily instruction)

Focuses on reading skills at sentence level. Provides exercise in five areas, Word Attack, Vocabulary, Literal Comprehension. Interpretive Comprehension and Word Study Skills. *(Course is suitable for remedial students)*

**CRITICAL READING SKILLS**: Grade 7+ (2 years daily instruction)

Helps develop advanced vocabulary and comprehension skills. A textbook contains 150 reading selections from such subjects as literature, science and history.

**FUNDAMENTALS OF ENGLISH**: Grade 7+ (2 years of daily instruction)

Provides instruction and practice in the formation of correct and complete sentences, nouns, pronouns, verbs and adverbs.

**COMPUTER LITERACY**: (.5 years of instruction)

Provides clear and nontechnical instruction to computers and computer programming for students who have little or no knowledge of computers.

** **Reports for the above mentioned computerized courses are available on request only.**

## ENROLLMENT

The number of students presently enrolled in the programmes at the facility are as follows:

| TRAINEESS | INMATES | MALE | FEMALE |
|-----------|---------|------|--------|
| 6 | | + | |
| 1 | | | + |
| 1 | | + (remedial) | |
| | 2 | | + |

All students are receiving computer-assisted instruction, and all students with the exception of one remedial student, are studying for the GED (high school equivalency diploma). With all the information provided, you will note that students have a volume of curriculum available to them for the enhancement of their educational development but for a short duration.

## RECOMMENDATIONS

Please note that the majority of the students (trainees/inmates) that attend class do not have a high school diploma. (A must in today's society.) Some dropped out of school, while others had learning difficulties while attending school. In order to assist these young men and women, helping them to be productive citizens, they need to be attending school (classes) on a regular basis similar to the programmes available in the public school system or private school system. On completion of their high school diploma, students need to be still active in their educational development by enrolling in Bermuda College or enrolling in correspondence courses. Education is an ongoing process. It would be beneficial and advantageous if these students attended class from 8:45 a.m. to 12 noon daily. Presently, approximately four (4) hours of instruction is insufficient. This includes the time the teacher and students reach the class. If you want to see positive results, realizing that some of the students were not accepted or had been rejected by the system due to behaviour problems and learning disabilities, it would be of further interest if all educational programmes be provided daily in the mornings. Afternoon classes can consist of art, health, vocational programmes, substance abuse education, physical education, counselling, sewing classes, trips to various places of interest, etc. The brain, especially in students with learning disabilities and lack of motivation, tends to function at its best in the morning. Afternoon activities will enable students to relax and not cause too much mental activity.

In closing, the mentioned programmes have been in the prison establishment since February 1984. A considerable amount of patience, endurance and caring has been put into the programme. Time which is immeasurable has also been incorporated having to spend time outside of the prison preparing lessons, preparing tests, and making photocopies and research for special projects. In all, there has been some success with over 200 inmates receiving instruction, 58 inmates receiving their high school diplomas (56 males and 2 females) over 150 inmates receiving computer education, 12 inmates released with better reading skills and approximately 6 inmates enrolled in university (higher educational programmes). As quoted by the Ministry of Education & Culture, **"Our schools are … striving towards excellence … every child a winner."** Let us remember these words … **"If you think that education is expensive, try ignorance!"**

**Submitted by:**
Neletha Butterfield
Computer Education Consultant/ GED Instructor
30th October, 1989

*Speaker's Chambers*
*House of Assembly*
*Bermuda HM 12*

Ref.:   GA-90-1

16th May, 1990

Ms. Neletha Butterfield
Prison Fellowship of Bermuda
8 West Park Lane
Pembroke

Dear Ms. Butterfield,

At the meeting of the House of Assembly on Friday, 4th May, 1990, Mr. N. B. A. Bascome, M.P., and Ms. J. M. Smith, M.P., asked that the congratulations and thanks of the House be sent to the Prison Fellowship of Bermuda for holding a Week of Prayer and including in their prayers Government and Justice officials.

In carrying out the wishes of the House, may I add my personal congratulations.

Yours sincerely,

HON. D. E. WILKINSON, M.P.
SPEAKER

*Her Majesty's Prisons*

*P.O. Box HM 264*

*Hamilton HM AX, Bermuda*

*In reply please
quote the date of
this letter and the
following reference:*

MISCFILE2

26th October, 1990.

Ms. Neletha Butterfield,
c/o C.A.R.E. Computer Services,
8 West Park Lane,
Pembroke, HM 07.

Dear Ms. Butterfield,

I am writing on behalf of the Inmates Programme Committee to thank you for the tremendous amount of time, energy, and enthusiasm you devoted in order to make the National Children's Week Activities at        Co-Educational Facility a success. All of us present were impressed by the excitement displayed by the participants.

We are most appreciative of your contributions to the development of the youth in our custody and look forward to continuing our productive relationship.

Sincerely,

Derrick S. Binns, Ph.D.,
Psychologist for Prisons.

:mej

cc: Education Officer

Speaker's Chambers
House of Assembly
Bermuda HM 12

Ref.:   GA-90-1

6th March, 1991

Mrs. Neletha Butterfield
G.E.D. Instructor
H.M. Prisons
P. O. Box HM264
Hamilton HM AX

Dear Mrs. Butterfield,

At the meeting of the Honourable House of Assembly on Wednesday, 27th February, 1991, Ms. J. M. Smith, M.P. and Mrs. G. A. Bell, M.P. asked that the congratulations of the House be sent to the Prison Officers, Teaching Staff and inmates of the Co-Ed Facility who brought out the talents of those in their care in a Black History Month presentation, "The Dream Lives On". Ms. Smith described the presentation as a most heart-warming and enlightening affair.

In carrying out the wishes the House, may I add my personal congratulations.

Yours sincerely,

HON. D. E. WILKINSON, M.P.
SPEAKER

# National Prayer Breakfast
## Congressional Executive Committee

POST OFFICE BOX 76440
WASHINGTON, D.C. 20013-6440

December 7, 1991

Ms. Nethlita Butterfield
Willowbank
P. O. Box MA 296
Sandys MA BX,
Bermuda

Dear Ms. Butterfield:

I have the pleasure of inviting you to join us for the 40th National Prayer Breakfast on Thursday, January 30, 1992, at the Washington Hilton Hotel. Your formal invitation and response card are enclosed.

Since our last National Prayer Breakfast, our country united in seeking God's protection and guidance during Operation Desert Storm. This year we join together to thank Him for answering our petitions and to seek guidance during this era of dramatic change.

An integral part of the Prayer Breakfast is the National Leadership Seminar which begins Wednesday evening (the 29th) with dinner and includes seminars, a luncheon and dinner on Thursday. These events add an extra dimension to the Breakfast and offer an opportunity for guests to share beliefs and concerns with friends from throughout the world. The cost for participating in the Breakfast and Seminar is $280 per person of which $150 is tax deductible. These funds allow us to invite a number of international guests, as well as some guests from our country who otherwise would not be able to attend.

In order to insure appropriate seating for the Breakfast, we need your response within two weeks of receipt of this letter. The enclosed room reservation card should be returned directly to the Washington Hilton Hotel no later than January 8, 1992.

The National Prayer Breakfast and Leadership Seminar offer us a special time to be together. We hope you can join us.

With best wishes,

Cordially,

Ted Stevens

Ted Stevens

COORDINATING OFFICES: PHONE (202) 546-1731    FAX (202) 544-0113

Not Printed at Government Expense

# WHAT HAPPENS TO PEOPLE IN PRISON?

- 90% of all people in prison are there because of crimes related to theft and substance abuse.

- The Priority Mandates given to the running of most prisons in order are:
  - Control of the prison population to keep them from society
  - Safety within the prisons
  - If possible, rehabilitation

- Because of these priorities, drug and alcohol problems lie dormant. Although most prisons take away the availability of abuse substances because officials have their hands full maintaining security, little or no drug abuse programs are available.

- In prison, there are repeat offenders and inmates. Inmates normally do anything they are told without complaint or rebellion. Repeat offenders complain and rebel most of the time.

- A convict or repeat offender's reputation becomes very important to him; after all, it is the only reputation he has.

- With these things in mind, prison becomes a place of total negative thoughts any delay or irregularity produces gigantic negative vibes. Dear John letters, more criminal charges; all news in prison is bad.

- Prison makes men very aware of failure. A man may fail many times, but he doesn't become a failure until he blames somebody else. Many prisoners blame others for being in prison.

- Prisoners go through the whole range of emotions. Trauma with fear, doubt, guilt, frustration, fantasies over wives and girlfriends. Also, a man's family is also sentenced to all kinds of social and economic hardships as well as shame.

- According to recent psychological reports where the average adult makes hundreds of mental decisions daily, the average inmate makes 30.

- When a man goes to prison, if he did not have psychological problems, then he is almost certain to develop them. Life is all downhill for a prisoner.

# WHAT HAPPENS TO THE AVERAGE PRISONER WHEN HE IS RELEASED?

- Most prisoners, as opposed to the popular view, leave prison in a state of depression not euphoria because of feeling inadequate, an inability to cope with the world outside and a feeling of alienation.

- Very few have caring families to return to.

- Some prisoners are literally met at the prison gates on release by ex-inmates—many times cured criminals—with liberal supplies of alcohol and drugs and women.

- Finding a job is difficult. Most employers will not even consider them. For men especially, self-worth is largely identified with their job.

- Any feeling of self-worth retained after incarceration tends to become further diminished by the inability to get a job. This results in deep depression or compensation with a fake show of self-worth with fancy clothes, flashy cars, women, drugs, and alcohol, which forces them back to crime to acquire the money to pay for these things.

- Some inmates become frustrated because, although they have good job skills, they are forced to take a dead-end job because they cannot find employment in their own field.

- It takes a released prisoner an average of six months to readjust to freedom of society; most do not stay free that long.

# WHY DO PRISONERS END UP BACK IN PRISON?

- Two out of three prisoners accept it as their home.

- According to U.S. prison records, 74% of prisoners released are back in four years.

- 80% of all crimes are committed by ex-offenders.

- Lack of employment and employment skills, including motivation, is the number one reason prisoners return to prison.

- Most prisoners have no home to go to.

- Few, if any inmates end up with friends outside the criminal environment.

# HOW CAN WE HELP EX-PRISONERS STAY OUT OF PRISON?

Since the main factors behind prisoners being incarcerated are low educational standard, lack of supportive home life or broken homes, and substance abuse, all these problems have to be addressed in a successful Rehabilitation Program.

- First, it is essential that first-time offenders be kept separate from those who consider prison home.

- The one problem that can be addressed in prison is low or lack of education standards.

- Existing Bermuda Prison Education programs are attended regularly by some inmates. Mandatory Education Reception (inmates should be questioned from childhood through adolescence).

- Learning vocational skills and the ability to use them when a prisoner completes his sentence are tremendously important. Bermuda has a tremendous market for vocational skills, especially with such a shortage of tradesmen. These skills can take a minimum of a year and sometimes longer to learn; they are particularly well suited for longer term prisoners.

- The dignity of labour is a key factor in reform and is something required as a daily diet.

- Helping ex-inmates with employment should be a major, if not, number one goal of correction.

- To do so, it is necessary to build community relationships with prospective employers.

  Finding hidden and obvious jobs, selling prospective employers on hiring ex-prisoners, and offering a good quality product in the men's labour are all important.

- Inmates will need to be trained how to prepare and act in interviews. It is important to teach punctuality, showing respect for authority, and doing a proper and satisfactory day's work.

- Men will need some counselling and help to return to society in areas such as these:

  Married men will have to be helped and reminded of the duties of being husbands and fathers. Men may have to relearn the skills of eating with families, how to be polite, how to behave in relations based on female friendships.

Also, men may need to learn how to face up to new fears and how to control their temper.

- When a prisoner is released, they will need a place to stay away from the influence of criminal involvement and, above all, they need the same as every other normal man —love, concern, shelter, security, and forgiveness.

# PRISON FELLOWSHIP RETREAT
# 1992 WASHINGTON, DC

29th January – 1st February, 1992

*"A bruised reed he will not break,*
*and a smoldering wick he will not snuff out.*
*In faithfulness he will bring forth justice;*
*he will not falter or be discouraged*
*till he establishes justice on earth.*
*In his teaching the islands will put their hope."*

—Isaiah 42: 3–4

On 7th December, 1991, I received an invitation letter from the National Prayer Breakfast Congressional Executive Committee to attend the National Prayer Breakfast in Washington DC on 10th January, 1992.

In conjunction with this prayer breakfast was the National Leadership Seminar held by Prison Fellowship International their annual retreat.

I attended this prestigious event along with Mr. Dennis Bean who prayed that God would open a door for him to attend, and his prayers along with others were answered. I truly believe because of Dennis's faith and his walk with the Lord, he was granted permission to travel.

**Words from Chuck Colson:**

*On behalf of the Prison Fellowship Board and staff, Patty and I want to welcome you to Washington, DC.*

*We're thrilled that you have joined us for this special time of fellowship and study. Your friendship and support are a personal encouragement to us and were looking forward to this time of getting to know you better.*

*We have tremendous opportunities before us during these next few days. We are particularly excited about our participation in an inmate chapel service at the medium security prison in Lorton, Virginia.*

*We pray that God will refresh our vision for this ministry and challenge us to see how we can better serve Him. Thank you for taking the time to be with us. We know that God will do great things in our lives in these days we are together.*

All events took place at the Washington Hilton Hotel commencing with the Prison Fellowship Retreat registration on 29th January and the Prison Fellowship Banquet in the evening.

The following day was the National Prayer Breakfast and, in the afternoon, seminars followed by dinner in the evening. Friday, 31st January, we did Bible study with Dr. W. Gary Phillips, prison visit training, prison visit, and dinner in the U.S. Capitol's Mansfield Room. A tour was given by Congressman Bob McEwen.

The last day, we had more Bible study lessons, and the retreat closed with a luncheon and the chairman's message by Chuck Colson.

A very memorable event especially witnessing the attendance of the President of the United States and Mrs. Bush, several senators, congresswomen, and congressmen, members of the PFI Board, and volunteers. To God be the glory – great things He has done to allow me to attend on behalf of Prison Fellowship Bermuda and my homeland Bermuda.

# SWITCHED-ON PRISONERS

9th April, 1993

*"The inside story on how inmates are upgrading their computer skills..."*

In the past eight years, as many as 90 past and present inmates of Bermuda's prisons have gained a high school diploma while behind bars.

Ten more prisoners at Casemates are preparing to sit for the exam later this year; they are able to do so thanks to CARE Computer Services and the educational programmes run at the prison.

CARE (Children and Adults Reaching for Education) was set up by Neletha Butterfield 10 years ago to promote computer literacy and give people a head start in the world of work. She began by installing a computer laboratory at her North Shore home and continues to run a busy school from this location today.

A programme to help prison inmates upgrade their skills using computers was started by CARE in 1984, and Ms. Butterfield now runs regular classes at Casemates and the Prison Farm.

She believes that in order to fully rehabilitate and prepare inmates for the outside world, it is essential to keep them abreast of technological developments in particular. "It is extremely important to keep the inmates in touch with the outside world and especially technology, which is changing so fast, if we are to rehabilitate them properly," she said. "Some of them are fathers, and they will need to keep in touch with what their children are learning in school these days."

The major problem confronting CARE and the prison authorities is the cost of computer equipment and the rate at which computers are becoming obsolete.

Ms. Butterfield, calling on the private sector to donate both software and hardware, said the prison would also welcome second-hand equipment tossed out by businesses in the process of upgrading their systems. "We do have one insurance company that provides some books and diskettes, and I would like to see more companies do so. What the employers have to realize is that these inmates, when they come out, will be looking for jobs, and jobs today are computerized."

With better equipment and facilities, Ms. Butterfield believes that a larger number of Bermuda's incarcerated could end up leaving the prison better qualified than when they went in.

## Call for More Up-to-Date Equipment and Teaching Support

The general feeling among Casemates prisoners taking the computer courses is a positive one, but more up-to-date equipment and teaching support are becoming necessary, they say. At the moment, they are relying heavily on teaching assistants, usually skilled inmates, and self-motivation.

Alan (not his real name) began working with Ms. Butterfield on computers four years ago. He had no computer or keyboarding skills when he started, but he is now designing programmes and has created five games for children and adults.

He assists the teacher and helps the students when she is working in the other classroom with the GED students. "I learned keyboarding skills, word processing, did my GED and got my 'O'-level maths and English as well," he said. "Most recently, I received a certificate for completing a micro-computer correspondence course."

Having learned basic computer programming skills under the CARE teaching scheme, he now reads books and magazines for new programming ideas. "I would like to get into repairing computer equipment and perhaps start my own repair business once I get out of here," he said.

The computer equipment available at the prison is used heavily and has to be repaired frequently. The two most modern models receive the most use, and Alan said he would be lost without the new Apple II GS. "I do all the statistics for the sports programmes in jail on it. Right now, I am working on the cricket schedule for this year," he said.

Another inmate has been waiting to join the computer studies group since he came to Casemates last June. The demand for places has been so great that he fears he may not have the opportunity to participate in the lessons before his time is up later this year. "Administration told me I could join the computer class if I agreed to do the GED, so I signed up for that. After a couple of months, I had heard nothing so I contacted the vocational officer. He said he would look into it, but then another couple of months went past, and I had still heard nothing, so I approached Ms. Butterfield." The inmate said he would like to see the class extended to embrace more prisoners and a volunteer teacher to assist Ms. Butterfield.

"The guys up here are being given the chance to further their education without having to pay for it, and that is a blessing to us. But when administration starts to provide something and then cuts it back, our hopes are dashed."

The number of students interested in attending computer classes at Prison Farm has dropped off because the equipment is limited.

Ben (not his real name) described Ms. Butterfield's presence as "astronomical" and believes the computer class would have "fizzled out" long ago without her encouragement. "This is quite a big class considering the facilities. There are really only two computers in the computer skills room that are up to date, so you can only use one for half an hour before having to make room for the next guy." Ben has been incarcerated for the past four years and has been attending computer class for the past three. He explains, "First of all, we had a summer class to introduce us to computers. There were around two dozen guys in the group, and we all passed. It was like an appetizer, and I felt like I was back at school and had that yearning to learn again. But the class is pretty stagnant right now because the software is so limited. We really need some more computers."

Rick (not his real name) has been taking advantage of the computer class to teach himself accounting and bookkeeping. "I plan to open up a business when I get out of here and will hire some of the inmates," he said. "Ceiltech is the name I've given the business which will deal in specialized cleaning for hygienic environments such as hotels and nursing homes. I have been planning this since I came in here two years ago. I am hoping this will be my last year. My wife sent me a user-friendly guide to accounting and running a business and that has been a great help."

Another inmate said he was particularly disappointed when Ms. Butterfield's Wednesday computer skills class was cut, but he has continued to teach himself. "I have been learning keyboarding skills," he said. "I am going to be in here a while longer, and I want to do something to improve myself. I've done five years and have got another five to do. I don't want to waste 10 years of my life."

# DEMAND SOARS FOR CLASS PLACES

Demand for places in the twice-weekly computer class as Casemates has increased dramatically, and attendance is "very good," according to Neletha Butterfield. The highest demand was recorded last year when the group was expanded from 15 to 25 participants. "The students are so interested that even when they have received their high school diploma, they don't want to drop out and make room for others," she said.

The computer studies course is just one of several courses provided for the inmates. Some of them have been upgrading their skills in other classes in preparation for the GED (General Educational Development) or high school equivalency diploma.

The Casemates computer studies group is divided into two sections: academic studies and a computer class. Academic studies comprising GED preparation, computer literacy, reading skills, problem solving, algebra, geometry, mathematics, spelling, and basic programming. The computer class allows students to improve on programming, word processing, typing, and accounting skills. There are 15 students in the first and 10 in the second, and the two courses are run simultaneously. The demand for the computer class has been so great that it has now been stipulated that students must first do an introductory course in computer literacy and the GED. "We encourage the students to take the GED course before going into the computer skills class," Ms. Butterfield said.

Four GED students were busily working their way through a variety of programmes at their terminals when a *Mid-Ocean News* reporter visited Casemates on Tuesday. All four have been participating in the study group for the past year. One has already passed the exam, and two will take it this summer. "One young man came in at 17. He has completed just about every course on the terminal and runs to class; he is so keen to get there," Ms. Butterfield said. These four terminals are hooked up to a central computer at Ms. Butterfield's North shore laboratory, and the users can access around 14 different programmes and study a wide variety of subjects.

CARE uses the Computer Curriculum Corporation, an integrated learning system used widely in schools across the United States. The information is automatically updated every six months, and the system also enables Ms. Butterfield to keep an up-to-date course report on each individual's progress. In total, Casemates has one Apple II GS purchased by the prison, an IBM-compatible PC donated by Prison Fellowship, and a further seven terminals belonging to CARE Computer Services. There are four other terminals at Prison Farm, also provided by CARE, and an Apple II GS provided by the prison.

This equipment is shared between the 25 inmates at Casemates and a further six at the Prison Farm. Although tuition is provided during two hours twice a week, the students only have a short period actually working on a terminal, and their time allowance is contracted further when computers are out of order. Breakdowns are fairly common because the equipment is in heavy use and a number of the computer will soon be obsolete, the inmates say. "We are only in class for two hours twice a week. The 25 students share the computer terminals and get about 40 minutes on a computer each session," Ms. Butterfield added.

The GED and computer skills courses were first introduced into the prison system nine years ago. Ms. Butterfield began with eight inmates at the former Senior Training School, a correctional facility for young male offenders, which has since been replaced by the Co-Ed Facility. "We were using personal computers at the time," she said. "I used to load them into my van and take them to the prison. The Casemates Facility heard about the class and how well it was going and wanted to participate. Classes began at Casemates in 1985. As time went by and technology progressed, we were able to bring computers in via modem, and we set up permanent terminals." She said that the courses are strongly supported by the educational officer at the prison, Nadene Lapsley-Dyer, and the vocational officer, Allen Richardson.

However, cutbacks because of financial constraints have hampered the computer study group, and some of the inmates say they have grown despondent. In addition to teaching at Casemates twice a week, Ms. Butterfield used to conduct a computer skills and accounting class on Wednesdays at the prison. The class is now run in conjunction with the GED group on Tuesdays and Fridays, and participants are having to rely more heavily on teaching assistants and working on their own.

"We also used to do accounting, typing and an introductory course to computing at the Co-Ed Facility in order to provide these women with some business skills, but the course had to be cut," Ms. Butterfield said.

But she believes the prospects for the prison computer course are not all doom and gloom. "I am hoping that when we move to the new prison, we will not only have a new building but some new educational tools as well," she said. "I believe strongly in the power of computers as educational tools and in using technology to provide motivating and interesting learning experiences."

Prison psychologist Dr. Derrick Binns, who heads up the transition team preparing for the move into the new high security prison nearby, said the finer details for a computer studies facility there have not been dealt with yet. However, the new building does have a computer room, and funding is being sought to equip it.

*Speaker's Chambers*
*House of Assembly*
*Bermuda HM 12*

Ref.: GA-91-1

3rd December, 1993

Senator Neletha Butterfield
C.A.R.E. Computer Services
8 West Park Lane
Pembroke HM 07

Dear Senator Butterfield,

At the meeting of the Honourable House of Assembly on Friday, 19th November, 1993, Ms. J. M. Smith, M.P., and Mr. L. C. Williams, J.P., M.P., asked that the congratulations of the House be sent to C.A.R.E. Computer Services on the celebration of 10 years of service in providing alternative education to Bermuda's children and adults. In making this request, Ms. Smith informed the House that over the years C.A.R.E. Computer Services had provided computer assisted instruction to over 1,000 young people and 250 adults, helping many to earn their high school diplomas, go on to further education or move to better jobs.

In carrying out the wishes of the House, may I add my congratulations.

Yours sincerely,

HON. E. D. DeCOUTO, J.P., M.P.
SPEAKER

# AN INSTRUCTOR'S MORNING
# IN THE PRISON

## 1997

*"As I walked out the door toward the gate that would
Lead to my freedom, I knew if I didn't leave my bitterness
And hatred behind, I'd still be in prison."*

### —Nelson Mandela

Friday morning and it's raining; the drive from Pembroke to Casemates Prison in Dockyard was difficult, but I arrived safely and dry.

It is 9:30 a.m. as I look through the dirty and stained window to acknowledge my arrival at the prison. The gatekeeper presses the button and the buzzer goes off to alert me that I can now push on the huge heavy iron door. By the way, there are two such doors. After a few pushes as the buzzer sounds again for the next door, it's not so hard to get through this one. With one push, I am through; slam again to ensure that the door is closed.

I pass through the visitor's area, "Good morning (uncle....) an inmate, a member of my family, and my mind drifts back over 30 years when I knew this individual as a child. Some of us as you know have family members doing time because Bermuda is a small place and from time to time, we will know of someone, a relative who is incarcerated.

I arrive in the gate lodge where the gate officer and a receptionist are. We all exchange greetings; I have to wait to be cleared to go over the hill for classes. It takes about 15 minutes as an officer has to leave his post up in the prison to come and escort me up the hill. While there waiting, an inmate approaches me and states that he has been waiting to get in my class. Is there room for one more? Sure, meet me in Section (1), and I will make sure that you enroll in class.

"Senator Butterfield," the Gatekeeper calls, "your escort is ready to take you over the hill." As always, the officer never wants to carry my heavy bag that is loaded with books and materials for the class. Why? Because it looks to feminine, and the inmates will tease him as he walks over the hill. This is soon overcome because of the weight and, of course, the officer is a gentleman.

The officer and I leave the gate lodge and start to walk towards the large gates with the smaller gate on the side of it. Another inmate who is working in the compound sings out,

"Good morning, teacher, looking lovely as always, anything for me in your bag?" he asks. I reply, "Sorry, just books of knowledge." As we near the small fence gate, with a sign above it saying, "Mind your head." The officer unlocks the gate, and we both enter one at a time with our heads bent down, for the gate is only about four feet high. We journey over the hill, not a bad climb today but, on a windy day, you have to walk backwards as the fierce winds within the prison walls blow you back downward.

No interruptions from inmates walking off the hill today because they are making time to court. There are several inmates at their cell windows singing out greetings. What a sight to see. We now approach section (1)—careful straight ahead, there are inmates getting a bath, shower, or wash from the basin. All this can be seen in clear view as there are no doors on the bathrooms or toilets. Towels are wrapped around them and, if there is no warning that a female teacher is approaching the section, you will see some birthday suits (smile). In Section (1), there is a booth with fencing and a door that inmates are not allowed to enter; they have to speak through the fenced window while the officers are busy rounding up the inmates for class. There are four sections of landings, and those inmates that are enrolled in class can be found on each of these landings. Patiently waiting as another 15 minutes of class time has gone by. The inmates approach Section (1) one by one.

While waiting for the rest of the class, the inmates wait in a hallway, eagerly ready to go to class. After all, they have been sitting or lying in the cells with some of them working in the kitchen and have to put down their tools to attend classes. As always, there is someone who wants a few minutes of your time. "Excuse, Ms. Butterfield. OOPS! I mean Senator Butterfield. Can I talk with you for a few seconds?" Well as usual a very depressing story.

Most of the students have arrived, and the officer has given the go ahead. Over 15 inmates and I are escorted by an officer to the class. Another fenced rusty gate to go through, down some slippery stairs and past the courtyard, where over 50 inmates or more are gathered in the courtyard for recreation, such as football, basketball, cricket, or just sitting and talking.

Every time I see this, my heart trembles to see so many handsome, healthy black men, who for some reason or another committed a crime or crimes. I say to myself they belong to someone. The courtyard is fenced in, and the cries of the men can be heard as I draw closer by them. Some would cling to the fence to say hello.

The officer unlocks another gate that leads to a classroom, library, and chapel. The students (inmates) now they are called because that is how they are addressed in class as students and I enter the gate and walk up a flight of stairs. As I approach the top of the stairs straight ahead, there is a chapel where today some lonely looking inmate is playing "Amazing Grace." Just what I needed to hear as my strength has been weakened by talking and listening to inmates, seeing inmates that I know, especially those who attended school with my sons. I turn to my left and I walk straight ahead, but I have to be careful because from the ceiling, water is dripping (not because of the rain). It drips all the time because of the dampness in the building (somewhat like a miniature Crystal Cave). There is newspaper on the floor to stop someone from falling or slipping down.

A few more steps—and the classroom is located straight ahead. Remember, it is raining, and panes are missing from the windows in the classroom. I believe the students are used to this, but I requested to have the windows stuffed with something to stay warm in the room. We ended up stuffing books from the library in the windows and some paper we managed to find.

As the students settle in their seats to begin class, you can hear inmates loud and clear in the courtyard. "Pass the f...... ball, you ...hole. Can't you f...... well kick." The profanity is something that is out of control, and it becomes part of their regular vocabulary. This goes on for the duration of the class, but somehow, we manage in the class to block it out and get down to our schoolwork.

"Good morning, class," and the students respond. Homework assignments need to be checked and, as usual, someone is worrying about someone else who hasn't completed their homework. "Mind your own business." You can hear this shouted across the small congested classroom. On this particular day, I was writing homework on the black board, and an argument broke out in the classroom. I dare not turn around and say anything, for there are times that it does get out of hand, very seldom though. No officer came to see what was going on, so I continued to write on the board in hopes that an officer would appear. Finally, enough is enough; I turn around as it is now time to end the class and ask the students to please stand, push their chairs in, and stand behind them quietly. I talk with them briefly letting them know that such behaviour will not be tolerated in my class. "Education is important, and you must get all you can; that is why you enrolled in this class to get your high school diplomas." By the end of this talk, the officer arrives to say our time is up.

We close in prayer, and everyone wishes me (the teacher) a good afternoon and a good weekend. Yes, we go back the same way we came. An inmate volunteers to carry my bags (what a different approach from the officer). You get so much respect from the students (inmates), and that is what teaching is all about, and it becomes very rewarding.

I am once again escorted off the hill by an officer, and the voices of the inmates from their windows can be heard again. "Have a great day, Ma'am." We arrive at the bottom of the hill, and you would think that by that time I'd be glad to be leaving, but it's Friday and the big black prison wagon is unloading the truck with inmates from the court downtown. From the back of the truck, out jump six inmates all handcuffed together. Reminds you of slaves being transported to the slave market for sale but, in this case, it is more goods to store in the warehouse of prisoners. In fear of taking a good look as to who they are, I say to myself, "Please don't let it be young men that have already been to prison and are returning." Sure enough, it is, and the tears start to roll down my face as they say hello. "Enough is enough," I say to myself, but I quickly remember that the system is geared this way, and society has not yet reached the level of thinking and accepting inmates back on the streets. I finally get the courage and have a few words with them—so young and so innocent looking. A young man in his early twenties asks me to pray for him. I am so overwhelmed by his request and strengthened by it because he wants help.

A morning in the prison for me is one of the hardest, heartfelt experiences that I encounter. Crime is on the increase; it is getting worse but, with God's help, we can do something about it. Young people must educate themselves and prepare themselves for the future and the future generation. If we have knowledge to share, let us light our candles and share with others allowing them to get a light from us, for we are our brother's keeper.

*Written by: Senator D. Neletha Butterfield, J.P.*

# TREATMENT OF OFFENDERS BOARD

## Annual Report 2000

*"It is said that no one truly knows a nation until one has been inside its jails. A nation should not be judged by how it treats its highest citizens, but its lowest ones."*

**– Nelson Mandela***"

*Excerpts from the report of the Treatment of Offenders Board Chairman in 2000. This report reflects the treatment of those individuals from society who are incarcerated serving their time in the correctional facilities.*

I am honoured to have this opportunity to serve as Chairman of the Treatment of Offenders Board.

The Board consists of new and former members who have both a wealth of experience and a broad understanding of all aspects of the community. It is my belief that the members who have served the Board well in the past, and together with the new members, they will serve the Board well in the future

Many challenges exist within the prison system. We welcome those challenges and the new initiatives for prison reform for the 21st century.

The Board supports the new initiatives and looks forward to playing a key role in helping to implement any changes that may result. We recognize that challenges and change may be threatening at times. However, it is my hope and prayer that we will not abandon our responsibility, but go forward to meet all challenges and change successfully together.

As Chairman, I wish to thank the Minister, The Hon. Paula Cox, J.P., M.P. for her confidence in my appointment to the Board. I am also thankful for the guidance and support I have received from the immediate past Chairman, Mr. Austin Thomas, J.P. and the Immediate Deputy Chair, Mrs. Marlene B. Landy, J.P.

As we continue to look ahead to 2001, I would like to thank all the members of the Board for their commitment, diligence and willingness to serve.

Let us continue to work in partnership with the prison establishment to give every inmate an opportunity to strive towards returning to the community as a positive and productive citizen.

## D. Neletha Butterfield, M.P.
## Chairman
## Treatment of Offenders Board 2000 General Observations

The Treatment of Offenders Board finds it extremely challenging to encourage inmates to do their best while incarcerated and when they return to society. Although, as indicated in past reports, the role of the Board is becoming increasing time-consuming, several members willingly remain beyond the scheduled time. The Chairman is most grateful for their time and commitment.

It is very rewarding to hear inmates express their gratitude for the many programmes that have assisted them in changing their lives and making positive decisions. Mention was made of the (SOP) Sex Offenders Programme and the (VOP) Violent Offenders Programme where some inmates found it very helpful. We are still concerned, however, about the limited skills that some inmates possess, and we note that this was due to a lack of resources for the vocational and trade training. We are pleased that this shortcoming is being addressed.

It is with deep concern that we continue to witness impertinence, disobedience, refusal to comply with prison rules and regulations, disrespect for prison officers, damage to prison property and use of abusive and threatening language to prison officers on the part of some inmates. There have also been several offences such as possession of unauthorized articles. Dishonesty continues to play havoc within the prisons as inmates steal from each other in addition to inflicting personal injuries.

Past reports have recognized the use of controlled drugs, and this is a real concern of the Board, to the extent that we have been examining ways to rectify this problem. The Board has zero tolerance for such behaviour. A strong message has gone out, and we are certain that this is being delivered. We support the prison authorities in their efforts to remain vigilant in order to curtail all unacceptable behaviour.

### Mental Health

This year we have witnessed a number of inmates coming before the Board in need of psychiatric treatment. It is our hope that in the near future, these inmates will get the assistance they need for their mental illness. We note this year that this concern was addressed by the Minister. It must be stated that the prison officers and staff are doing their best, and we salute them for their sterling efforts to help these individuals.

### Drugs in Prison

As noted in the general observations, the use of drugs is a real concern for the prisons as well as the whole community. Members have suggested that we take advantage of the use of modern technology in the detection of illegal substances together with a dedicated dog handler who is trained in the interdiction of drugs.

We must all come together and be very serious about the problem and begin to address it. We look forward to the Alternatives to Incarceration initiatives because we believe that this will address the drug problem and establish programmes that are high on the agenda. Far too many years have gone by and the question remains: Why is it so difficult to stop drugs from being detected in our prisons? The drug detection techniques, prevention and education programmes are continuously being reviewed.

We commend those inmates who are addicted to drugs and those who take steps towards rehabilitation by joining the drug educational programmes. We wish them every success; it is an ongoing process to be drug free. We also want to commend those who take advantage of the drug prevention classes to improve themselves because they understand the consequences of continuing to make negative decisions.

## Prison Violence

This year, the prisons noted an increase of violence within the correctional facilities. The Prison Officers Association expressed this concern in November of this year. We are concerned for the protection of all officers and staff members and again state that the Board has a zero tolerance for violent threats and offences committed against those placed in authority. We would like to express our gratitude to those prison officers who continue to play a significant role under difficult circumstances. We believe that it is only through their dedication and professionalism that they have been able to overcome some very difficult situations.

We acknowledge that the violence in the prisons is a reflection and a reality of what is happening in our community today. The Violent Offenders and Anger Management Programmes are in place and must be used to the fullest extent. If inmates are to become productive members of society once released from prison, it is important that they learn to curb their violent behaviour while incarcerated.

## Prison Reform

In December 2000, Government announced the Alternatives to Incarceration (ATI) Initiative. This initiative is a move from a predominately punitive system for criminal justice offenders to one based on rehabilitation and restorative justice. This prison reform is an integral component of the process of developing tough and mandatory programmes for inmates.

In addition to ATI, legislation is now in effect to control the activities of convicted sex offenders once they have completed their prison sentences. Concern is usually at the highest when high profile sex offenders are released from prison. This has been a concern in the community, and society has to be protected.

## Civil Inmates

There has been an increase of civil inmates housed in the general population. Some of the civil inmates have been separated and housed in the F building adjacent to Westgate Correctional Facility to reduce overcrowding. It is hoped that in the near future, and alternative facility will be found to house them. With the increasing number of civil inmates who come before the Board for various reasons, the Board recommends the appointment of an Administrative Assistant. He/she will attend to the various administrative needs and problems that occur and the present prison officer can then be re-assigned to his prison duties.

## Prison Plant

The Board has had the opportunity to visit the various prison facilities on numerous occasions on a regular basis. The conditions of the Prison Farm are unacceptable and the Board has reported this in the hope that changes will be coming soon. The other two facilities are in need of maintenance and we are certain that these too, will be addressed in the near future.

## Volunteer Services

The Board acknowledges the many individuals who have contributed to the rehabilitation of inmates, restoring in them a ray of hope and the joy of being loved. We commend the volunteers for their time, skills and commitment to serving in this way and for touching the live of the inmates. Whether it is for church, recreation, educational development or as guest speakers and mentors, these volunteers have made a difference in the inmates' lives. Many on the outside may criticize, but the work that is performed voluntarily inside the prisons is outstanding. If more of us chose to volunteer, we would make a significant contribution to society and further the cause of healing mankind.

## Education

The Board notes that this area is very significant due to the many challenges facing the community in the workplace. We note that many of the inmates have taken advantage of the educational programmes available and several have achieved many certificates of completion, too numerous to mention in this report. The results are available.

Inmates are to be congratulated for their achievements and each year a prize giving ceremony is held at the Co-Ed Facility to recognize their accomplishments.

When inmates come into the prison system, they are screened for their educational levels and in some instances, case plans are recommended. Several inmates coming before the Board have not completed high school and some have serious difficulty with reading, life skills and social skills. It is important that these concerns are addressed immediately and appropriate programmes put into place along with assessment and progress reports.

If we do not address their need for education and survival skills, inmates will return to society without the ability to cope and function as productive citizens. It has been stated that education is the passport to one's future and that the future belongs to those who prepare for it today. Those persons who are incarcerated must acquire a desire for education and skills training based on an understanding of the benefits they will provide for them in an ever-changing society and workplace.

We hope that the inmates in the Maximum Security unity will also be given the opportunity to participate in educational programmes and activities. Inmates in this unit spend too much time doing virtually nothing. The policies for this unit need to be reviewed as soon as possible to avoid the frustration and aggravation displayed by long-term inmates.

The Board applauds those teachers and instructors who give of their time and skills to enhance and encourage the inmates.

**Prison Reports**

Reports for each inmate are made available to the Board from the following sources:

- Police Report
- Chief Officer's Report
- Probation Officer's Report
- Prisoner's Representation
- Medical Report
- Chaplain's Report
- Educational Report
- Prison Social Worker's Report
- Assistant Commissioner's Report

The reports are read aloud for every member to hear immediately before the inmate is presented to the Board. Whilst this is a time-consuming process, members accept it because of the valuable information in each report.

These reports enable the Board to make decisions that are best suited for the inmate. On many occasions, inmates are very remorseful and display a readiness to move on with their lives and make a positive contribution to society. There are those that cannot be recommended for work release and if successful, release on license because of mental illness, poor attitudes towards programmes and an unwillingness to change lifestyles.

The Board notes that those who continue to return (high recidivist) state that they are tired. However, many have not made any adjustments to their present lifestyle.

Some members of the Board feel a sense of hopelessness when they see inmates, hear their voices and cries and watch them wipe the tears from their eyes while relating their past history of sexual abuse and drug abuse; for example all members try to participate by offering personal assistance and words of comfort. Truly some of these cases are a startling reflection of the society ills that are all too prevalent in our community.

The Board has on several occasions requested that all reports from professional staff be typed, due to the difficulty of understanding individual handwriting. This request has been fulfilled and has enabled the Board to process the reports much more efficiently.

## Acknowledgements

## Probations Services

The Board recognizes the invaluable contribution of the Department of Probation Services. Regular attendance of Probation Officers at the meetings is to be commended. Mrs. Gina Hurst-Maybury and her caseworkers have been of great assistance with extensive reports on individuals committed to their charge and responsibility. Their recommendations and probation orders have been invaluable. These individuals are professionals who go beyond the call of duty making sure that those released in their care comply with the probation orders. The probation reports identify the inmates' home environment, social environment, employment status and capabilities and recommendations for housing, counseling and after care drug and sex offender's programmes. The Board is aware of the Department's heavy caseload in addition to the stress that they must encounter with so many difficult cases. The Board salutes the professionals at Probation Services for their undying efforts and wishes them the best as they strive to meet the increasing demands of the courts, prisons and other services requiring their assistance.

## Retirement

The Treatment of Offenders Board acknowledges the years of dedicated service given by Westgate Correctional Facility officers; Calvin Butterfield, Stephen Dean, Charles Fox and Alfred Robinson, all of whom recently retired from service. The Board wishes them well in all future endeavours and thanks them for their loyalty to the Bermuda Prisons Department.

## Appreciation

The Board appreciates the assistance provided by the Minister, the Permanent Secretary, the

Commissioner, the Deputy Commissioner, Assistant Commissioner, Chief Officers and the prison staff. The accomplishments of the Board were possible through their assistance and care. We thank them for their kindness and support.

We thank the officers and kitchen staff of each facility for the homemade refreshments, displaying their culinary arts and skills at each of our meetings. Their presentations have not gone unnoticed. We truly appreciate the quality of service at each meeting.

The secretary, Miss Toniiae Smith, as always, has done an outstanding job of taking the minutes of some very lengthy meetings and discussions. We thank her for her expertise in the recording and presentation of our minutes and other secretarial duties relating to the Board.

We appreciate all the hard work and support that so many have given on our behalf and acknowledge that we all play an important part in changing lives and building a better community together.

*The full report was tabled in the House of Assembly and placed in the parliamentary library for reading and review.*

# PAROLE BOARD

## 7th July, 2000

*"Specialist parole board mulled, as prison numbers rise"*

Talks on the need for a specialist parole board are expected to gain ground during the summer. The board would replace the current Treatment of Offenders Board (TOOB), chaired by PLP MP Neletha Butterfield, and she told the *Bermuda Sun* she is in favour of the change.

The need for a specialist parole board has been well documented: In 1997 the TOOB, in its annual report, spoke of substantially increased workloads and increasingly hostile offenders. Then chairman Austin Thomas wrote: "Over the last 25 years, the role of the TOOB has become extremely heavy and difficult, it must be noted that crime and the criminal have become more sophisticated. The attitudes of those incarcerated and the legitimate concerns of society have changed considerably. "Clearly, the laws and regulations under which the TOOB conducts affairs needs to be updated and brought in line with the role such bodies play in modern penal systems."

Asked for an update on the situation Public Safety Minister Paula Cox said: "The Treatment of Offenders Board fulfills a very good function but I think that it would be useful to consider moving into a parole board which is then very much in sync with some of the amendments such as the Criminal Code Amendment in terms of sex offenders legislation and also the alternatives to incarceration project, where you are looking at risk management, risk control, and risk measurement; I still have an interest in pushing that forward."

She added, "It would be premature pending a Cabinet decision and me talking to the Treatment of Offenders Board after I've had Cabinet's authority to go very far in explaining the details of that."

# WHILE SOME INMATES LOOK FOR EDUCATION, RATHER THAN ESCAPISM

An educational course in African Studies is proving to be a big hit in the island's prisons. It is one of several courses being offered by CARE Computer Services, run by the former chairman of the Treatment of Offenders Board (TOOB) and PLP MP, Neletha Butterfield.

Ms. Butterfield quit the TOOB post when she realized it might conflict with her desire to interact with prisoners on an educational level, something she considers crucial in the fight against recidivism.

She told the *Bermuda Sun* "It was an honour to serve on the TOOB but during my tenure I noticed that the educational side of prison life was still lacking."

Ms. Butterfield acknowledges current programmes, but said that in order for her to feel she was "really assisting," she had to think about how she could "reach those I hadn't reached before." The answer was to implement the courses she offers at CARE into the prison system.

So far, courses include a GED preparation programme, computer studies, mathematics, and English. But it is the African Studies class that is attracting the most attention.

"It's been an overwhelming success," Ms. Butterfield said. "More than 30 have registered for the class."

In her TOOB Annual Report, which has yet to go before parliament, Ms. Butterfield, like her successor Austin Thomas, warns about the high incidence of drug use in prisons, but she believes it can be countered by instilling a sense of pride and dignity in young black men, which, she says, is achievable through courses like African Studies.

"These individuals have to find out who they are," she said. "It's about reawakening the African mind."

Lecturer Dr. Muriel Wade Smith wants to see African Studies on the public school curriculum. In the meantime, she is happy to be given the opportunity to enlighten inmates.

"It's the whole identity question," she said. "We have to respect that Africa is the cradle of civilization and the origins of mankind. We have been lulled into unconsciousness so much so that we have not recognized that we have been put under a white supremacist system – we are not conscious of that. We are ignorant of our past."

Asked whether she thought some people would be offended by that outlook, she saidthat after 23 years of not being able to get a job in her own country, "I really don't care."

Dr. Smith, who was Bermuda's first qualified international curriculum coordinator, said local history will also find its way onto the prison programme, something she believe should also be taught more in schools.

"Our young people are coming up thinking the exempt companies built this country," she said. "If we look around us today, our culture is virtually non-existent."

According to a spokesman for the education department, African Studies is included in the school curriculum at all levels.

She said: "The primary school curriculum, which is now being piloted for formal introduction in 2002, includes African Studies in social studies as part of global awareness and celebrating diversity."

She added: "At the middle and senior school levels, students study the Egyptian contribution to mathematics. In multicultural science with mathematics connections, they use African-themed games such as building model Egyptian houses, measuring height and geometry of pyramids.

"In the Arts, students study the African connection in dance, music, visual arts and theatre."

By Nigel Regan
*Bermuda Sun*
2nd November, 2001

Casemates Prison
Ireland Island
10/3/86

8 West Park Lane
Pembroke West
Bermuda

Dear Mrs. Williams,

I write with hope that this letter finds you and your family at your best. Last week seem to have been like two weeks in one, and will describe your absence as if myself and others had lost our best friend, or more like a broken romance. "Smile"

Your presence at Casemates has made Tuesdays and Fridays two special outstanding days behind these walls, and I like the others have become addicted to your warm and sound attitude. I've also found out that we are not the only ones that depend on your appearance, because, when talking with the Commissioner last week, he spoke very good of you and Deputy Commissioner Fraser, upheld you with high esteem, and how your ins and outs at P.H.Q. are solid. Commenting how your interest for your students at the prison being priceless and genuine.

I know and accept that you have a very wide scope to cover, and do understand that you are only human, therefore, I have added you in my prayers, that the good "Lord" bless, guide and protect you and that all good things come on to you.

May love peace and understanding be with you.

Always,
Your Student
Cleveland M.
Simmons

Wednesday, 20<sup>th</sup>
September, 2006

To the Hon. D. Neletha Butterfield, JP, MP
Minister of Education and Development

Thank you for the kind, inspirational, but further more encouraging words you sent me. Thank you also for the quality time you put in with me and more importantly for all the good work that you continue to contribute to the people of Bermuda. It will not go unnoticed.

Thank you once again and may this day be as good for you as possible.

Sincerely,
Calvin Trott

Morning Miss Williams,

Please forgive me for not attending class today. I sincerely beg your forgiveness.

I'd like to take this moment to thank you for all that you've done for me and the special attention you've had in me. May God bless you for being such a wonderful and caring person. Have a peaceful and blessed holiday. Bless you and your family.

Love
Kevin

Dear Ms. Butterfield,

Let me start by saying a thank you very much for the card which you took time out of your so busy schedule to send to me.

First of all, Ms. Butterfield, I want you to know that my decision to remove myself from your class had nothing at all to do with you. You see Ms. Butterfield, I have a lot of problems and I can't give you the full one hundred percent of my attention because they're always on my mind, so I feel its in my best interest to try and sort myself out first and then I may be able to deal with more important things.

You see Ms. Butterfield, all my life I've been hurt by people over and over again. I was nineteen when I was arrested on this charge. I was engaged to a very wonderful girl and out of that relationship of five years come my daughter and then the problems that I didn't know how to deal with, and then come the pressure and after the pressure came the explosion.

Anyway Ms. Butterfield I hope that you can now understand me and my plight, and once again thanks for the card and for being a friend and the best teacher that I've ever had.

Love, Denzil

Matthew 25:32–40:

*And before him shall be gathered all nations: and he shall separate them one from another as a shepherd divideth his sheep from the goats:*

*And he shall set the sheep on his right hand, but the goats on the left.*

*Then shall the King say unto them on his right hand, Come, ye blessed of my Father, inherit the kingdom prepared for you from the foundation of the world:*

*For I was an hungred and ye gave me meat: I was thirsty, and ye gave me drink: I was a stranger, and ye took me in:*

*Naked, and ye clothed me: I was sick, and ye visited me: I was in prison, and ye came unto me.*

Then shall the righteous answer him, saying, Lord, when saw we thee an hungred, and fed thee? or thirsty, and gave thee drink?

When saw we thee a stranger, and took thee in?

Or naked, and clothed thee?

Or when saw we thee sick, or in prison, and come unto thee?

And the King shall answer and say unto them, Verily I say unto you, Inasmuch as ye have done it unto one of the least of these my brethren, ye have done it unto me (KJV).

# LETTER OF COMMENDATION TO THE EDITOR OF THE ROYAL GAZETTE

20th April, 1987

Dear Sir,

I am very happy to see that your newspaper on 20 April, brought to the public's attention, the dedication displayed by Ms. Neletha Williams, with regard to the time she volunteers in teaching basic English and maths to the inmates of Casemates Prison.

I had the honour of meeting this lady while canvassing in Pembroke West Central during the last General Election.

I truly hope that the business community and Government will help fund the computer classes as it is a great step toward rehabilitation.

I also commend those inmates for trying to educate themselves while incarcerated.

Keep up the good work!

Cheryl Pooley-Bibby
Smith's Parish,
Bermuda

# THE BEST-WORLD'S GREATEST TEACHER

Your heart is pure
Your thoughts are fine
Of all the teachers
I'm glad our mind

Wisdom resteth in your heart
Good thoughts rest in your mind
Two words to describe you
Conscious and divine

You are a virtuous woman
Your price is far above gold
I hope God never stops feeding
Your body and your soul

When things get rough
For your family and you
Have faith in God
He will see you through

You are a great teacher
Your show dedication
I hope that one day
I could show appreciation

I could be feeling sad
I could be feeling blue
But after leaving your class
I feel as if brand new

**Princeton Robinson**
**4th November, 1988**

# CONCLUSION

*"I always tell my students that Malcolm X came both to his spirituality and to his consciousness as a thinker when he has solitude to read. Unfortunately, tragically, like so many young black males, that solitude only came in prison."*

**—Bell Hooks**

The words above were repeated over and over to my students behind the prison walls, especially the young black males at the Senior Training School back in 1984.

I worked for approximately 20 years in the education department of three correctional facilities travelling from St. George's to Dockyard three times a week having to leave one end of the island to get to the next correctional facility. Commuting was not easy, but I understood the importance of recidivism or the risk that another inmate would return to prison if I didn't try to make a difference.

I never thought that I would end up in prison, teaching of course, so I want to humbly thank my family especially my three children who when younger thought I was insane and was going to get hurt or injured by a prisoner. Let me categorically state that it was the best of times and that I enjoyed my teaching experience behind the prison walls immensely. It takes a lot of commitment, dedication and perseverance as an educator to overcome obstacles presented in a prison environment. Some in the community do not feel it's worth it until you see how many prisoners are eager for education to better their lives.

It is my strong belief and knowledge that prisoners look to their teachers as the only people who have not given up on them, believe in their abilities and earn their respect. I personally found them easier to teach than students in the traditional school classroom because they were committed to their education. This is to be noted throughout my book for there are so many success stories and the record of 150 inmates receiving their high school diplomas is a testament of their success.

*Education for the Soul behind the Prison Walls* highlights some of these accomplishments from the GED programme to computer training. I am very thankful and grateful to those who assisted me along the way, in particular the prison department, administration and correctional officers *(too numerous to mention)* who helped me in the past, the present and prayerfully will continue to help me in the future as I continue to volunteer my teaching services. The vision over 35 years ago is still being fulfilled behind the prison walls. May this collection of stories, letters, poems and words of gratitude touch your SOUL as you read my account and encourage you to also touch the lives of those who need our help both academically and spiritually beyond the prison walls.

# ABOUT THE AUTHOR

## HONOURABLE D. NELETHA BUTTERFIELD, M.B.E., J.P.

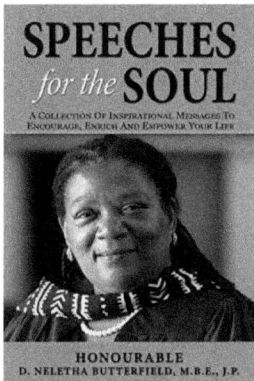

The Hon. D. Neletha Butterfield M.B.E., J.P., is the founder, owner and director of a computer school and an alternative learning centre called C.A.R.E. which stands for Children and Adults Reaching for Education. She founded the learning centre and computer school in November 1983.

The Hon. Neletha Butterfield represented the Bermuda Progressive Labour Party (PLP) in the Pembroke West Central constituency as a candidate in the 1993 General Election. She was appointed to the Senate by the Progressive Labour Party on 8th October (her birth date) where she was the spokesperson for Education, Community and Cultural Affairs, Youth Development, Sports, Parks and Recreation and Women's Issues. The general election of 9th November, 1998 she successfully won a seat to the House of Parliament after a decade of work in the constituency of Pembroke West Central.

She served as an opposition senator in the Senate from 1993-1998 and as a Government Member of Parliament for Pembroke West Central from 1998-2012. She brought to parliament her expertise, experience and enthusiasm in assisting those in the community and her country Bermuda. She sat in the House of Parliament as a Government "**back bencher**" from November 1998 – October 2002. She was appointed for the first time in 1998 by the Premier, the Hon. Jennifer Smith, DHumL, JP, MP to the executive board of the Commonwealth Parliamentary Association of the Caribbean, the Americas and Atlantis region as Bermuda's representative, a position she was reappointed to in 2008 by the President of the Senate, the late Hon. Alf Oughton and retired from this executive position in December 2012.

On October 8th, 2002 (her birthday again) she was appointed to the Cabinet by Premier Smith as Minister without Portfolio, spokesperson in the House of Assembly for the Ministry of Housing and a Justice of the Peace.

In the election July 24, 2003 she retained her seat in constituency %18 Pembroke West Central with an overwhelming victory in the new electoral districts. She was re-appointed to the cabinet by the Premier, the Hon. W. Alexander Scott, J.P., M.P. as the Minister of the Environment and on 2nd September, 2006 Premier Scott appointed her as Minister of Education and Development. In the change of the PLP leadership in October 2006, the newly elected Premier, the Hon. Dr. Ewart F. Brown appointed her on 30th October

2006 as the Minister of the Environment, Telecommunications and E-Commerce, a portfolio she held until December 2007. With approximately 20 years of dedicated service, commitment and expertise to the legislature, she proudly returned to the Government back bench from December 2007 – June 2009. She was re-appointed to Cabinet as the Minister of Culture and Social Rehabilitation on 23rd June, 2009. In another leadership change on 1st November, 2010 she was appointed as the Minister of Government Estates and Information Services under the Cox administration until 31st October, 2011. She now has retired from the political arena after 20 years of service to her country and spends some of her time in Jamaica where she finds peace and solace writing her memoirs.

Some of her achievements and accomplishments while serving within seven (7) cabinet ministries are highlighted:

***2004 :*** Bermuda Costal Erosion Report ***(Hurricane Fabian aftermath)***

***2005 :*** Community Areas Programme (CAPS) - *William F. Wilson Park* – ***Pembroke***, *Ladies Chamber Park* – ***Pembroke***, *Pig's Field Park* – ***Pembroke***, *Harlem Heights Park* – ***Hamilton Parish*** *and Olive Bank Park* – ***Warwick***.

***2005 :*** Bermuda Aquarium Museum and Zoo (BAMZ) bus

***2006 :*** Bermuda's first State of the Environment Report

***2010 :*** Formation of the Women's Council to focus on Women's Issues

***2011 :*** Cisco Network Academy at the Bermuda College

As a single mother of three whose own pursuit of education as an adult enabled her to provide for her family, she understands the importance of a sound education. She has dedicated her life to educating as many Bermudians as possible. She is a computer education consultant, a former Computer Lecturer for the Government Community School, a former lecturer at The Bermuda College in computers, English and mathematics and a former instructor of mathematics, reading, African studies with the Bermuda Correctional Facilities education department, in addition to teaching the GED programme that she introduced to the prison system for the first time in 1984.

In the thirty-five years since C.A.R.E. started, she has helped more than seven hundred and fifty adults obtained high school diplomas and assisted over 4,000 young people in computer assisted instruction and training. She has also used her talents to help inmates at the Prison Farm, Casemates Prison, Coed Correctional Facility and Westgate Correctional Facility, where one hundred and fifty inmates received their GED (high school diplomas) and over three hundred received basic education skills and computer training. As the founder of the General Education Development (GED) programme and the computer programmes in the correctional facilities, in 1985 she held the first graduation ceremony in the prisons and through her vision the educational programmes and graduation ceremony continues to be held annually and she currently volunteers her time teaching the G.E.D. Programme to inmates. She has also tutored young men from Reachout Rehabilitation Centre, His House, The Residential Care Centre, Focus Counseling Services, Turning Point, young women from Fair Haven, Teen Services and the Brangman Home and both men and women from Addiction Services. In June 2010, she held the first graduation class for Life Skills Programme to recovering addicts.

September 2002, her business C.A.R.E. Learning Centre enrolled for the first time from the Ministry of Education and Development, thirty (students) from CedarBridge Academy and The Berkeley Institute in an alternative education programme called **"Project Success"** for young teenagers.

She is the President of the Bermuda Business and Professional Women's Club, member of the Pembroke Community Club, Western Stars Club, the co-founder of Prison Fellowship Bermuda and a founding member of S.T.A.R. (Supportive Therapy for Aids Victims and their Relatives), Past Vice-President of the Orchid Charity Club, a steward and a former coordinator of both the singles and prison ministry and a former trustee at St. Paul A.M.E. church. She was a former chairman of the Treatment of Offenders Board and the Historic Building Advisory Committee, a former commissioner of the Board of Telecommunications and chairman of the Joint Select Committee on Education in the House of Assembly.

She was voted **Bermudian of the Year in 1988**, in 1989 received the **Community Service Award** from the Bermuda Business and Professional Women's Club, in 1993 the **Outstanding Service Award** for her community involvement from the Kiwanis Club of Hamilton and in March 1994 received **The Best of Bermuda Gold Award** for her outstanding work as an educator. February 24th, 2002 during Black History celebrations, she received from the National Association of Negro Business and Professional Women's Club, Incorporated **(Bermuda Club)**, the highest honour given to a woman, **The National Sojourner Truth Meritorious Service Award** for her meritorious community service and her deep concern for and participation in all activities advancing the status of women.

Known as "Honey" Butterfield she is an energetic community worker and educator who is much in demand as a public speaker both in Bermuda and internationally. Her overseas speaking engagements have included the Delta Sigma Theta Sorority, Washington D.C., The Computer Curriculum Corporation, California, The People's National Party (PNP) Women's Movement, Jamaica and the National Association of Negro Business and Professional Women's Club, Inc., Washington D.C., the House of Lords United Kingdom and QKingdom Ministries, New York and the Commonwealth Telecommunications Organization - Geneva, Switzerland.

In February 2004, the Hon. D. Neletha Butterfield, was inducted into the International Association of Business Leaders.

The following year February 2005, she was selected out of 7,500 well qualified nominees for the *"International Association Business Leader of the Year 2005 Award"*. She received this international award on 19th March 2005. The following week 26th March 2005 the Hon. D. Neletha Butterfield received another international award **"Women of Great Esteem"** from the QKingdom Ministries, New York. On November 26th, 2006 the Grace Methodist Church of Bermuda during the 100 Women in White Service presented her an award in recognition of her outstanding **"Community Service"**. On February 27th, 2009 she received an award from St. Paul A.M.E. – Hands of Faith Ministry for her **"Community Involvement and her support to the Ministry"**. In the 2009 Queen's Birthday Honours and Awards she was awarded a **M.B.E. (Member of the British Empire)** for her contribution to community education and her work for over 25 years in Her Majesty's Prisons. On the 4th September, 2009 by the Women's Integrated Network presented her with the **Bermuda International Women's Leadership Award** and on 5th September the "Lifetime **Achievement Award". On 8th March, 2011**, during the 100th anniversary celebration of International Women's Day she was honoured as one of **Bermuda's 100 Women of Vision. Certificate of Appreciation** – West Pembroke Pentecostal Assembly 2013. **Chautauqua Award** presented on 22nd June, 2018 at the YPD Conference Branch of the African Methodist Episcopal Church iRock Awards. On the 23rd March, 2019 the Rochester Genesee Valley Club of the National Association of Business and Professional Women's Club recognized her as the **International Literary Artist** honoured guest. Her most recent award was received on 7th April, 2019 **The Crystal Butterfly Literary Award** from the Atlantic Publishing House.

As a woman of strength and perseverance, it is through her trials and tribulations that her personal philosophy is based on the scriptural text in Romans 8:28 – *"All things work together for good, to them that love the Lord and are called according to His purpose"*. Her belief is that, *"If you can give an individual a fish, he has food for a day, but if you teach him how to fish he has food for a lifetime."*

Because her educational foundation was obtained in the Bermuda public school system, she believes strongly that the Bermuda public schools must be kept viable. Many of her interests and skills for what she has accomplished came during her early years and feels honoured by the establishment of C.A.R.E. in 1983 an alternative learning centre and computer school.

She states *"To God be the glory great things He has done and to the village that raised me and made me who I am today"*.

Hon. Butterfield has recently become an author and has published and released seven books,

*"Speeches for the Soul"*, *"Workshops for the Soul"*, *"Political Beginnings for the Soul"*, *"The Soul of a Community Leader"*, *"17 Trailblazers Who Walked with Purpose"*, *" Study Skills for the Soul"*, and *"Educating the SOUL Behind the Prison Walls"*.

She will soon release next year two new books entitled; *"The Soul of C.A.R.E."* and *" Students Essays for the SOUL"*.

She is the mother of three children, Jeffrey, Kirkland and Bry-Letha, grandmother to ten grandchildren, one great-grandson Sai'et and four great grand-daughters Neveah, Navi, Amyah and Rhylee.

# *Also by the author:*

## SPEECHES FOR THE SOUL

*A Collection of Inspirational Messages to Encourage, Enrich and Empower Your Life.*

## WORKSHOPS FOR THE SOUL

*A Collection of Educational Workshops for Motivation, Training and Upliftment*

## POLITICAL BEGINNINGS FOR THE SOUL

*A Collection Of Speeches, Writings, Conferences And Interviews Highlighting My Political Journey*

## THE SOUL OF A COMMUNITY LEADER

*Educator, Senator, Parliamentarian, Cabinet Minister - A Historical Journey*

## STUDY SKILLS FOR THE SOUL

*The Tree of Life on the Legacy of the Visionary*

## 17 TRAILBLAZERS WHO WALKED WITH PURPOSE

*The Bermuda Business and Professional Women's Club Sojourner Truth Awardees 1967-2002*

*Available on Amazon and other booksellers*